Decoding
BOYS

New Science Behind *the*
Subtle Art *of* Raising Sons

Dr Cara Natterson

First published in Great Britain in 2020 by Yellow Kite
An imprint of Hodder & Stoughton
An Hachette UK company

First published in the United States in 2020
Published by arrangement with Ballantine Books, an imprint of Random House, a division of Penguin Random House LLC, New York

1

Copyright © 2020 by Cara Natterson

Book design by Elizabeth A. D. Eno

A CIP catalogue record for this title is available from the British Library

Trade Paperback ISBN 978 1 529 33983 3
eBook ISBN 978 1 529 34132 4

Printed and bound in Great Britain by Clays Ltd, Elcograf S.p.A.

Hodder & Stoughton policy is to use papers that are natural, renewable and recyclable products and made from wood grown in sustainable forests. The logging and manufacturing processes are expected to conform to the environmental regulations of the country of origin.

Yellow Kite
Hodder & Stoughton Ltd
Carmelite House
50 Victoria Embankment
London EC4Y 0DZ

www.yellowkitebooks.co.uk

For Ry, who gave me the gift of being mom to a son.

For Talia, who understands her brother in ways amazing to me.

For Paul, who is the better half of both of the above.

And for my mom, who raised three boys. In hindsight, I've got mad respect.

Contents

Introduction

DECODE: to convert (a coded message) into intelligible language; to discover the underlying meaning of; to understand what the heck is going on here.

Puberty's jumble of feelings and behaviors, not to mention physical transformations, can be downright confusing to its recipient adolescents and bystanding parents alike. That's nothing new. But over the past couple of decades, girls have tackled puberty head-on, mainstreaming conversations about body parts and completely destigmatizing their biological and emotional metamorphoses. All the while, boys sat quietly on the sidelines.

The net result is that girls own puberty. Not all of them, but many. They talk about body changes, emotional swings, friendships, and family dynamics; they use words that used to be R-rated (*vagina! periods!*) freely. When they start to show signs of entering womanhood, the world now hands them a microphone so they can talk and talk and talk.

But not boys. They tend to slink into this stage of life surreptitiously, helped by the fact that their bodies generally don't announce the massive shifts within—there are no zits or bulging muscles—until years later. And they get quiet, or at least quieter, than they used to be. Many parents take their sons' newfound silence as a clear indicator that they don't want to talk, and in an effort to respect this shift, or maybe just to keep the parent-son relationship on solid footing because it's what sons seem to want, we say okay and stop attempting to engage them. Bye-bye, deep conversations about most things puberty-related. The shift is subtle at first, but by the time our boys' voices crack and hair sprouts in their armpits, many parents know very little about our sons' lives, and have often lost the ability to ask. The upshot is that we actively leave boys out of the very same conversations we pull girls into.

Even if you communicate with your son, the world in general doesn't. Sure, our boys are warned about the bad things that can happen to them if they engage in certain behaviors (usually related to sex, drugs, or a baseline level of stupidity), but they don't get a fraction of what the girls get. Beyond basic management of hair and stink and growing testicles, no one talks to them about the paradoxes of this stage of life, like the fact that they often just want to go quiet, but can also have rage; they have deep thoughts but are also impulsive; they grow and develop later than girls (at least many of them), but are steeped in a culture of violence and sex at increasingly young ages. All of this is confusing, to say the least, made more so with our relative parental silence. But the real consequence is to arrive in adulthood unprepared for much of what is expected of them.

If only our boys could experience what our girls do: endless streams of content in every direction covering not just what's happening to their bodies and brains but also the precipitators and upshots of their behaviors, including (but certainly not limited to) sex and drugs and violence. Maybe, just maybe, our boys would then enter the world as young adults armed with more knowledge, which in turn could protect them from dire consequences. And eventually, as they grow older, they would pay it forward, decades from now parenting their own children with more open dialogue, evolving into a generation of future fathers who take on these same conversations with their kids comfortably and eagerly. If only, right?

I say they can. It's just up to us, today's parents, to move the dial. And that means starting conversations.

If this book were two sentences long, here would be the text in its entirety: Despite what they say ("I'm fine"; cue closing door) and despite social convention (if he doesn't want to talk about it, leave well enough alone; "He's fine"), *not* talking to your son about his evolving physical, emotional, and social self is the biggest parent trap of them all. Because if *you* don't have the conversations, someone else will: a friend who's got it all wrong, or a family member who doesn't exactly share your ideology, or the Internet with its endless treasure trove of image-based content, presenting still pictures and videos that, once viewed, your son can never un-see.

I come to this particular subject matter—and my mild fixation on making right the wrong we inadvertently do to our boys—in a thoroughly roundabout way. Back in 2011, I had just signed on with the juggernaut toy company American Girl to update their cult-classic puberty book *The Care and Keeping of You*. That same year, the book itself had just become a teenager, marking thirteen years and three million copies in print. It should go without saying that the book was written for girls. For clarity's sake, I did not write the original book, though I wish I had: every pediatrician I knew told every parent of a tween girl to go out and buy it, because its cartoony innocence and straightforward, girl-friendly tone made for the best basic health primer available. By speaking to younger girls before they even began their journey to womanhood, *The Care and Keeping of You* filled a void left by the go-to body book that preceded it, *Our Bodies, Ourselves*, which was a lot of things—part feminist manifesto, part biological encyclopedia, and part doorstop (all 647 pages printed on 8.5" x 11" paper and weighing in at what felt like ten pounds)—but it wasn't meant for young girls with very basic questions.

In 2011, I got to work updating the original *Care and Keeping of You* and creating a follow-up book for older girls creatively titled *The Care and Keeping of You 2*. But at the same time, I also became super vocal about a boy book. In fact, from day one with American Girl, I pitched *The Care and Keeping* for boys (nicknamed by one of my closest friends *The Care and Keeping of Dudes*). Even during the process of being vetted for a dream job to update and expand a wildly best-selling book published by a company that *only makes things for girls*, I risked imploding the opportunity by telling everyone I met at American Girl how there had to be a parallel book for boys.

To a person, they all looked at me like I was insane.

But, I insisted, it's the same book—just minus the pages about female anatomy and periods. All kids deserve information about taking care of their hair, how to brush their teeth effectively, why nail-biting and zit-popping are bad ideas. In fact, eighty of the one hundred pages of *The Care and Keeping of You* aren't even about being female and growing up; they are about being human and taking care of your body and soul. The book destigmatizes questions about health, wellness, and physical transformation by covering sleep and exercise, friendships and family dynamics, not to mention a whole lot of hygiene. What about any of that is exclusive to girls?

Year after year, I got back the same replies from American Girl: *That's a great point. Totally get it. You are so right. But nope, not going to happen.*

In 2013, *The Care and Keeping of You 1* and *The Care and Keeping of You 2* launched to great fanfare. They debuted on the *New York Times* bestsellers list, and one or both remained there for more than two hundred weeks, falling off only when the category (Middle Grade Paperback) was eliminated. My editor, mom to a tween son and deeply enthusiastic about the future prospect of a boy book, called me to share the good news that the series was expanding again.

"Boy book?" I asked with bated breath.

"No, sorry. But a mother-daughter book. Third book in the series. It'll be great!"

At this point my own son was turning eight, the entry point into the tween demographic. The irony was not lost on me. My books, because they are published by a toy company, have age ratings just like toys sold in stores. Everything I have written for American Girl is rated for age eight and up. My then ten-year-old daughter lived in the *Care and Keeping* demographic sweet spot, but my son, aging into that target demo, had nothing waiting for him. I went to the three last remaining bookstores in Los Angeles (that's a deeply depressing topic for another time) and furiously searched Amazon's online library. I bought every boy book out there, and it's worth noting there were only four of them. While each offered good information, they were either text-heavy or dry or chaotically organized. Not one did what seemed obviously necessary: to be an age-appropriate and appealing voice of clarity about body changes, sure, but also to cover simple things like the virtues of washing with soap in the shower, why sports drinks are no different from candy bars, and the value of communicating with your parents.

So I decided to take matters into my own hands. I called publishers with whom I had worked in the past, before my American Girl days, and others whom I'd met while traveling on book tours. Infused with the confidence that they would want to publish a best-selling author's book filling a gaping hole in the market, I took meeting after meeting. *Nope. Sorry. Not gonna happen.*

The big argument against me was that there existed no track record: the sales comparisons for boys' body books held no sway because so few parents bought them. (*That's because they aren't great books that do what they need to do!* I argued. Didn't matter . . .) And there's no shelf for them. There's barely a girls' health section in any given bookstore to begin with, but there's *definitely* no boys' health section. (Um, first of all, there are essentially no bookstores in existence anymore, so the whole shelf argument seems moot. And when a good product doesn't exist, how can the argument against it be that a good product doesn't exist?!) I was flabbergasted. They were each polite in the way they said no.

My son turned nine. There was nothing to give him. I did a book signing for the *Care and Keeping* books and a mom asked me to sign a copy to her son.

"You do know it's a girls' book, right?" I asked.

"Of course I know," she said, "but I will just clip the pages in the middle about the hoo-ha and the periods and give it to him because he needs to know how to floss and why his feet smell!"

As an aside, I have always thought of *The Care and Keeping of You* as a great book series for boys to read in order to learn about girls. So much so that I had planned to show it to my son down the road, when he was ready to learn about rudimentary girl anatomy and biology. But it took another mom to point out to me that the rest of the content I so desperately craved was all right there for him—granted, presented in a book that's pink and purple and packed with illustrations of only girls. But who cares, I thought. Information is information.

Then I got a call that shocked me.

"Go!" said my editor.

"Go where?" I replied.

"Go write the boy book, before we change our minds." It was almost five years after I first came to American Girl.

In the summer of 2017, American Girl launched its first-ever boys' product: *Guy Stuff: The Body Book for Boys.**

And I suddenly became fluent in the conversations around

---

* Okay, full disclosure: American Girl had also launched a boy doll, earlier in 2017. But according to all marketing materials and everyone I know at the company, the doll was not targeted exclusively—or even at all, according to some—at boy audiences. The company was not trying to reach out to boy consumers who they hoped would buy dolls. Rather, the boy doll, Logan, was simply part of the American Girl family, meant for girls and boys alike, just like all of their other doll products. So, *Guy Stuff* really does get credit for being the first American Girl boy-directed product.

Also, while we're talking credit, my son deserves full credit for the title of that book. When I asked him what it should be called, he paused for a second—maybe two—and said, "*Guy Stuff*, because that's the only book I would read." He would have added "duh" if he had the energy.

boys coming of age. Or the lack of conversations, to be more precise. Which is, ultimately, my point. The story of my uphill climb to publish a book about basic health and hygiene—and we are talking basic!—was really a tale about shining a light on the fundamental difference between the ways we talk to our girls and to our boys. When girls tip into puberty, they often become increasingly verbal or at the very least more emotionally transparent. Our culture reinforces this by acknowledging it, celebrating it, and marketing to it. Girl puberty, with its moods and curves, is patently obvious. While *The Care and Keeping* series sells widely, it sits on a crowded bookshelf competing with a dozen other titles aimed squarely at girl audiences. The same scene plays out across all media platforms, from TV to film to digital to print. Over time, this glut of girl content has morphed into female empowerment movements and "leaning in." It has elevated teen girl culture.

Maybe it was the increasing loudness of girl conversations that finally shed light on how little we talk to and about our growing boys. Or maybe it's the general sense that puberty conversations are a limited quantity. The sex talk used to be called The Talk, and parents reveled in its one-and-done-ness. Today, we have moved beyond this (thankfully), recognizing that we need to have many conversations about a wide variety of issues over lots of years. But it's almost as if there is a social rule that the amount of talking we—parents, doctors, educators, advocates, magazines, movies, blogs, vlogs—can do is finite, and so the more we talk with and about and to our girls, the less there seems to be to go around for our boys. Information is not a pie, though. It is not a limited resource that is carved up until it is gone.

Which is the long version of how I landed here. My wish was granted—I published a book for boys about what was happening (or going to happen or had happened) to their bodies so that they could have a springboard from which to talk with their parents. But in filling one hole I found another one, perhaps much larger: following our sons' leads, we too pivot to silence. And that is what this book aims to call out and course-correct.

This is a book about parenting boys through their adolescence, starting from the age of eight or nine and extending into their early twenties. It's a look at the dramatic shifts boys face physically and mentally (covered in Part One, what I call the "Inside Changes") and emotionally and socially (Part Two, the "Outside Forces"), filtered through my medical and child development lens. I probably cover too much ground—everything from early puberty to late blooming, body image to gun violence, sex ed to sexual assault—but there was nothing that seemed cut-worthy because parents constantly call me, email me, stop me and ask me for the information contained within these pages. *Decoding Boys* is ultimately your guide to a snapshot in time: What is happening to our boys as we raise them, and how can we raise them given what is happening?

With a bird's-eye view, I will walk you through the experiences of many. But because so much of my content represents an average or typical course, at some point while you are reading you will inevitably think: *That's not true,* or *That doesn't sound like my kid.* Which is fine—anticipated, actually— because a book that is a couple of hundred pages long covering nearly two decades of development in a rapidly changing society cannot possibly describe every variation. Not to mention that our bodies don't read the textbooks. They do what the heck they want, when they want to, in a uniquely and genetically prescribed order and, of course, heavily influenced by their environment. If there is anything I have learned from my twenty years as a pediatrician, it is that "normal" can express itself in many different ways and there are a million qualifiers, special circumstances, and asterisks influencing this normality. So there isn't one path across puberty, not even a set order of steps through which the body morphs from its child to adult form. I expect you to shake your head from time to time.

My goal is to light a conversational route through puberty

and adolescence while acknowledging that everyone travels a slightly different road. The experience of raising your son (or your daughter, for that matter) depends upon a long list of variables: both of your temperaments, similarities, differences, strengths, challenges, genetics, socioeconomics, opportunities, family structure, and on and on. This doesn't mean, though, that we don't share multiple common threads. Clearly we do. To begin with, every parent I have ever met says that raising safe and healthy children is their primary goal.

The chapters that follow dive into topics we all know we need to think through. They can be so big, though, so overwhelming that we want to plug our ears and *la-la-la* our way past them (that's how I felt while I was writing . . . often). The reality is, we can't. Because if we do, we will leave our sons vulnerable to temptations that put them at risk for consequences that will shift the trajectory of their lives, usually not in good ways. Understanding boy puberty and the timing of maturation arms you with insight into your son's current life experience. Thinking about topics like boy body image, access to pornography, and gun violence will empower you to begin the conversations we all need to have with our sons.

Here's what this book is not. First, it's not a biology textbook. I will give you lots of physiological information—especially in the back of the book, which is essentially a mini course in Puberty 101—but if you want to dive deeper, there are other great resources referenced, including some specific to mental illness, which is a sprawling issue that can make a dramatic debut appearance during the tween and teen years. I encourage you to access these sources, because the more robust your knowledge of how the body and mind operate and why they morph the way they do during this stage of life, the better you will understand what your child is experiencing. Don't rely too heavily on your recollection of high school biology—our understanding of what is actually happening inside the body during this transitional period continues to evolve, and your old "facts" might be very wrong. Frankly, most of us don't even remember our own adolescence accurately, we only carry with us a reel of highlights and lowlights.

This book is also not the be-all and end-all. It documents the thinking of one person, ideas built on data and facts, medical training and firsthand life experience, thousands of conversations, and countless hours in exam rooms and classrooms. But I am the first to acknowledge that I am one of many voices. We each have a lens, and I use mine to tie together pieces of information in order to help you rethink one element of your life: the parenting part. Please don't mistake this, though, for the presumption that I believe I am the last or only word on the topic of parenting boys.

So this isn't a textbook, it isn't a be-all and end-all, and finally it isn't a statement on gender or emerging sexual orientation. There is much to discuss about these topics, to be sure, but puberty happens to everyone, independent of the gender with which they identify or whom they crush on and fall in love with. This book begins with an explanation of being genetically male impacts the physical and perhaps emotional journey; as it unfolds, it is about how we might rethink our parenting strategies in light of this biology. However, focusing on the typical heterosexual and cis-boy experience does not—and should not—minimize the relevance of physical change and cultural pressures on people who identify otherwise. I hope it is clear that the forces at play in today's world impact all kids, regardless of their gender or their sexuality, and by association all parents.

In order to decode boys in the throes of puberty and have a hand in shaping them into the men we hope they will be, we need to be ready and willing to master a small amount of biology, see our sons through a newish lens, and let go of the idea that we completely understand what our kids are going through—because our transformations happened a long, long time ago in a thoroughly different world. And then, as we do with our girls, we need to open the conversational floodgates. Ultimately, I have come to believe that in order to parent our boys best, we must get over the notion that silence is golden. We wouldn't—we don't—tolerate our girls shutting their doors and shutting us out, because *she needs to know*. Well, it's time to start raising our boys more like we raise our girls. If there's one thing you will realize while reading this book, I hope it's that *he needs to know, too*. And that means we need to talk to them, even when our sons go quiet.

Decoding
BOYS

Part One
INSIDE CHANGES

Chapter One
HOW TO TALK TO BOYS

IF BOY PUBERTY HIRED A MARKETING firm to design a logo, it would be an image of a closed door; if it were animated, the door would be slamming.

Someone once told each and every one of us boy-parents that isolationism was a normal guy thing, and we collectively agreed to accept it. So when boys enter puberty and slowly begin to shut out the world, we parents tend to let it happen. And then they emerge out the other end as men (or man-boys at the very least) and we think, *Who is this guy and why don't I know very much about what makes him tick?*

We can't decode our boys if we don't talk to them, even though that's precisely what many of us tend to do: *not* talk to them. Testosterone and other naturally produced chemicals may have a hand in making our sons retreat, but our own parental keep-the-peace, give-'em-what-they-want, be cool strategy of silence just breeds more silence. It is time for all of us to let go of our preconceived notions that our sons don't want to talk.

And so, welcome to the end of the book offered up at the very start. Usually, precious bullet-pointed nuggets of summary appear at the end as reward to the reader for having made it through data, anecdotes, and pages of waxing philosophic. Not here. I am flipping that structure because it makes no sense to hold out on you. If you have talking tools at your disposal, then as you read through these chapters you can dive in with your son on any of these various bits and massive pieces of puberty, sex, drugs, and all the rest when they are fresh in your mind. In other words, read these couple of pages and there are no more excuses for delaying the conversations.

So, without further ado, here's how to talk to boys about puberty and the enormous physical, social, and emotional shifts that go along with it. The shortest first chapter you may ever come across in a parenting book, ideally as helpful as it is brief. And spoiler alert: every single one of these tips applies to girls, too.

HOW TO TALK TO BOYS

1. START TALKING! Take any discomfort you may feel about any of the subjects in this book and multiply by 100. That's how uncomfortable your son feels. So get over your jitters. In order to open up dialogue with your kid, you will need to start the ball rolling. That means talk. Out loud. To him. Even if you are dying inside.

2. LISTEN. When guys are ready to talk—for some it happens a lot sooner than for others—listen. And ask questions, too. These are the easiest ways to avoid dominating the conversation. Don't just dispense wisdom (no matter how genius you believe your advice to be) but actually ask what he thinks, because you may learn something.

3. AVOID EYE CONTACT. At least in the beginning, find ways to have conversations that don't require you to stare down your kid. The car is an ideal place for this because, ostensibly, your eyes are on the road and he's nowhere near your direct line of sight. Ditto that moment when you say good night and flip the lights off— literally not seeing one another can open the floodgates. Or pick your own favorite time and place to make believe the person you are talking with is not actually there. It's a great icebreaker. It also largely explains the runaway success of texting and social media.

4. TURN OFF DEVICES. Speaking of what happens on screens . . . If you're trying to have a moment here, make sure that your son's eyes aren't glued to one. You'll never utter anything more deep or meaningful than what's on the phone in front of him.

5. GRAB TEACHABLE MOMENTS. You don't have to make an appointment with your kid to have a meaningful talk. And nothing bad needs to have transpired. Just grab a teachable moment anytime it pops up: when you are watching something together and you see cringe-worthy behavior, point it out; when a bus drives by with a completely inappropriate ad that you cannot believe is even legal, talk about it; when someone is walking down the street in a plume of vapor that smells like mango, point it out rather than pretend it doesn't exist (and for those of you who don't know where that fruity cloud came from, that's vaping). Use other people's behaviors—both good and bad—to illustrate to your own kids what you expect from them. They may return the favor by pointing out *your* habits, so try not to get annoyed.

6. EXPLAIN WHY WITHOUT LECTURING. Every time you make some blanket statement or rule, follow it with a short explanation of why. You are not apologizing—rather, you are providing a rationale so that your kid can actually take your rule outside of your house (or even just your line of sight) and adopt it. "No" is indeed a full sentence, but "No, because . . ." is a far more effective one. Keep it brief, though, to avoid falling into the pit of serially lecturing your kid, because this breeds silence, sometimes fear, or it's just plain tuned out. Back-and-forth dialogue is the key to successful parenting. So avoid monologues and instead make almost every conversation a two-way street.

7. BE PATIENT. In order to win at parenting through puberty, have many talks over many years, and take these conversations slowly. When a conversation goes quiet—which it will—ride out the silence by practicing the art of letting your kid break it when he's ready to speak. If he seems perfectly happy sitting in silence, pepper him with occasional questions or keep adding little bits of information until he says, "Okay, got it, we can stop." Or until he literally leaves the room. That happens. It's fine.

8. POINT OUT THE BRIGHT SIDE, BUT DON'T OVER-PROMISE. Puberty is awkward, at least some of the time. It can make a big difference if you point out the parts that are proceeding slightly more seamlessly. For instance, if your son is struggling with bad acne but has started his growth spurt and doesn't have any insecurities about his size, you may want to mention the advantages of his height. Or, if you have a perfectly complected petite guy, underscore the upside of his clear skin. The goal is not to throw some other kid under the bus, but rather to remind your own child that there may be some elements of this journey he is taking for granted. Puberty is the ultimate game of "the grass is always greener."

That said, remember that puberty is fickle, and something that is not an issue one day may suddenly become one the next. The tallest boy in sixth grade may find himself shorter than average in the long run; the guy with the perfectly complected face might discover a giant crop of "backne." Don't get burned by this. The grass *is* sometimes greener.

9. FIND YOUR SURROGATE. There are going to be some things your kid just doesn't want to talk about with you. That's normal, so plan for it. Talk to your son about who else he can go to for advice on the important stuff. Ideally, identify someone you both trust, and that someone should have at least a few years on him—his same-aged best friend is not ideal for the part. Here's a really important caveat: tell the appointed person! Prepare him or her and even share what you hope they will say in specific circumstances. There's nothing worse than being surprised by your go-to status in the middle of an emergency.

10. AND FINALLY, TAKE DO-OVERS. Perhaps the most valuable piece of advice on the list, it's not about talking to your son as much as talking yourself off the ledge. If you screw up—which we all do—own it and pivot. We will make mistakes, bring our children to tears, set rules that are nonsensical, say things we don't mean, laugh at the wrong times, punish disproportionately, miss the things that really needed discipline, roll our eyes in a less-than-subtle way, wear our hearts on our sleeves, yell, not yell, and make every other mistake in the book. We're human. When you make the wrong call, set the wrong rule, or react in the wrong way, take ownership, apologize as necessary, and then give yourself another chance. Take the do-over. That's called being a parent.

Chapter Two
UNDERSTANDING TESTOSTERONE: THE MAGICAL HORMONE THAT TURNS BOYS INTO MEN

TESTOSTERONE HAS A REP TO PROTECT. It's responsible for aggression and risk-taking, muscle bulking and flexing. Got rage? Blame T. Science backs these claims, with study after study demonstrating that testosterone indeed deserves a fair amount of credit for the biology behind the amped-up, aggro male. Testosterone, though, isn't a one-trick jacked-up pony, and this narrow reputation often overshadows the wide variety of roles it plays.

Testosterone sits at the center of maleness in every way, responsible for much more than bulk and belligerence. It (and its derivative cousins) bear responsibility for the formation of male body parts in the developing fetus; triggering boy puberty, not to mention advancing boys through it; sex drive and its accompanying erections; bone density and red blood cell production; and male-pattern baldness, too. While testosterone is not a lone actor—it leans heavily on a cascade of other naturally produced chemicals to seal any given deal—it is integral to all of these processes and a slew of others. So in a book about how boys morph into men, the natural starting point is an in-depth look at the hormone that seems to play a role in almost every corner of maleness.

This chapter describes how testosterone works and why it is

so central to physical maturation and the making of men. It also dives into how, if at all, testosterone impacts the way we connect with our sons. Because almost every parent of a newly minted teenage boy experiences some degree of retreat: verbal, physical, oftentimes both. They shut their doors more often, their conversations with us dwindle, and eventually many move to a repertoire of single-syllable answers ("yeah," "no," "okay," or just a flat-out grunt). There certainly exist boys who do not fit this description—and girls who do—but even the chattiest boys will typically go through a period of relative silence. Boy quiet is a phenomenon so common it deserves a spot on the formal list of what to expect when they're developing, somewhere between new-onset foot reek and eating you out of house and home. But is this a side effect of T?

While there have been hundreds of studies looking at testosterone's effects from fetal life through old age, this primer will save you from reading all of them. Here is your summary of testosterone's magical effects on the body and what we know to date about its role in classic boy rites of passage.

ELEVEN PARAGRAPHS OF BASIC SCIENCE (AND THEN YOU'RE DONE): WHAT IS TESTOSTERONE?

Welcome to the most basic facts about testosterone described in a relatively unscientific way, because no one should feel intimidated by understanding how the body works. Simply put: testosterone is a hormone responsible for the structure and function of boy parts and more. A *hormone* is a chemical naturally produced by the body that regulates the activity of cells or even entire organs. Humans have lots of different hormones managing lots of different processes. For instance, thyroid hormone regulates how energy is expended; growth hormone makes the bones (and other things) grow; and insulin, the hormone made by the pancreas, manages sugar levels throughout the body. People often think hormones all connect to puberty and eventually sex, but that couldn't be further from the truth—most hormones have absolutely nothing to do with either of these.

But testosterone *is* largely about sex and genitals. Manufactured by the testicles (hence the name . . . get it?) beginning in fetal life well before birth, the very presence of testosterone—and the ability for the rest of the body to "see" that testosterone via receptors on the outside surfaces of different cells—makes a boy a boy. Any human fetus that does not adequately produce or sense testosterone will become anatomically female.

After infancy, testosterone lies low for several years. Small amounts of the hormone are produced in scattered spots outside of the testicles: some comes from the adrenal glands (which sit atop the kidneys in both genders); and some is *peripherally converted,* which means that there are hormones floating around the body that look a lot like testosterone but aren't exactly testosterone, and these can be transformed (aka converted) into testosterone by certain tissues such as fat (which sits in the periphery of the body). There are studies suggesting that T may rise for a short spell in the first year or two of life, but for all intents and purposes, it exists in very low doses until boys hit their tweens and the hormone begins to surge. From then on, the testicles are the main production sites of testosterone, accounting for 90% of the male body's T supply.

Boy puberty begins when a specific region of the brain, the *hypothalamus,* releases a hormone called GnRH (short for *gonadotropin-releasing hormone*). This hormone travels a short distance within the brain to another area called the *pituitary,* which responds to GnRH with the release of two different hormones, LH (*luteinizing hormone*) and FSH (*follicle-stimulating hormone*). LH and FSH leave the brain and take the long trek south to the testicles, where they turn on the testicular machinery, stimulating production of testosterone and eventually sperm.* The new higher levels of testosterone in the blood-stream signal a switch in the hypothalamus, telling it to stop releasing GnRH; this then stops production of LH, FSH, and eventually testosterone too, causing T levels to fall. But as soon as testosterone hits a low enough point, the hypothalamus is then switched back on and again releases GnRH, which again stimulates LH and FSH, which tell the testicles to kick back on their testosterone-making apparatus, and the cycle begins anew. It's a well-orchestrated routine of positive and negative feed-back loops, turning on and off the release of various natural chemicals made by different parts of the body.

There's debate over what exactly prompts the initial rise in GnRH, instigating the whole puberty process in the first place. In fact, nobody knows precisely why our kids start to develop. But what is clear is that puberty resets the brain's sensitivity to testosterone. Preschool-aged boys live with low levels of circu-lating T, but their brains don't tell their testicles to make the hormone even when levels are barely detectable. Meanwhile, pubescent boys and adult males have much higher (up to fifty times higher!) levels of T circulating through their bodies and when the levels dip just a little bit, they start making more. So heading into puberty somehow resets the testosterone sensitiv-ity meter in the male brain. On a related side note, here's a fun fact: guys and girls both make testosterone, and it's key to a

---

* Some hormonal detail for those who are curious: LH is responsible for turning on the production of testosterone, while FSH stimulates the growth of the *seminiferous tubules*, the sites of (future) sperm production. If testicular growth is the earliest sign of puberty—a fact that is covered in great detail in Chapter 3—then FSH gets credit for making the testicles actually grow, be-cause it is the enlarging seminiferous tubules that account for most of the in-crease in testicular size.

And while we are footnoting, it is also worth pointing out that FSH and LH are the very same hormones responsible for tripping girls into their puberty. In girls, these hormones travel to the ovaries, where LH turns on estrogen pro-duction and eventually ovulation, and FSH turns on the machinery that will begin to ripen eggs one at a time through a woman's fertile period.

whole bunch of bodily functions in both genders. This T is produced in the adrenal glands and fat tissue. But the testicles churn out testosterone starting in puberty, and since girls don't have testicles, this accounts for why males are suddenly so much more flush with T than females.

In case you haven't run across a list of what testosterone actually does in the body, skim this one. Mostly because it explains pretty much everything your little boy will face as this hormone makes its presence known. When testosterone levels get high enough, you will see:

- growth of the penis and testicles (this one you only *might* see, depending upon how private your son has become)
- sex drive and erections (ditto *might*)
- increases in lean body mass and musculature
- deepening of the voice
- new or exaggerated personality traits, particularly ones related to power and dominance

Now, you may have noticed the absence of hair and acne on that list, and this is because testosterone isn't the only puberty hormone in town. As boys transform into men, some of their pubertal changes are actually thanks not to testosterone but to other hormones produced in the adrenal glands, the so-called *adrenal androgens*. The terminology tends to get cumbersome, so here's the most basic info you need to know: *androgen* is the name given to any "male"* sex hormone, so testosterone falls

---

* Androgens in general and testosterone in particular play roles throughout the body, way beyond male secondary sex characteristics. Testosterone is important in metabolism, bone health, liver function, and the brain, too. In fact, many people take issue with calling T the "male" hormone—especially recently, in the world of sports, where testosterone levels are used to define whether a person can compete as a female. The case of Olympic runner Caster Semenya is drawing a spotlight here. When female athletes have naturally high

under the androgen umbrella. The adrenals make a bunch of different androgens, hormones like DHEA, DHEA-S, and androstenedione. Some of these are weaker hormones that essentially act as stepping-stones for the others; some have powerful effects in their own right; and some can be converted into testosterone in remote parts of the body.

Adrenal androgens are the primary reason all kids, boys and girls, start to get greasy, hairy, and stinky. They have a direct effect on the hair follicles, changing the color and texture of the hair that emerges from them—hello, pubic and armpit hair!—and increasing the amount of oil and sweat pumped out through the follicles as well. With increased oil and sweat production comes body odor. Much more on all of that in the back of the book, but the reason I mention it here is that testosterone is often wrongly accused of causing hairiness and stench—these features are largely the fault of the hormones made in the adrenal glands, not the testosterone produced in the testicles.

Which brings us to one interesting side note about puberty in general and testosterone in particular: even though growing hair and becoming sweatier or greasier are classic signs of puberty, they are consequences of the adrenal path, not the testicular path. And this means that when kids do start to have body odor or sprout pubic hair, even though they have some mature adult body features, these are *not* signs that they are becoming reproductively mature. It's only when the testicles mature in a boy (or the ovaries in a girl) that a kid becomes capable of making a baby. So if you do notice that your child has a lot of hair down there but there's nothing else going on, he's in a form of puberty called *adrenarche* (see the word adrenal in there?) but not in *gonadarche* (from *gonad*, aka gamete-producing organs: the testes and the ovaries) and so he's not really in full-fledged puberty yet.

testosterone levels, does this give them unfair advantage? Gender distinctions and definitions across sport are increasingly debatable.

Testosterone has tremendous impact on various body parts, but it is counterbalanced by the female hormone estrogen. Just as testosterone is mostly made in the testicles, estrogen is largely produced in the ovaries, and since guys don't have ovaries you would think that's the end of the story. But again, just as testosterone precursors can be manufactured in the adrenal glands and converted in the peripheral tissues, so too can estrogen. So males have low levels of estrogen in the exact same way that females have low levels of testosterone. When estrogen levels rise too high and there is a hormonal imbalance, males can have some feminizing features. The most common is *gynecomastia,* or what many guys like to call "man boobs." In boys these are usually small and temporary—they can look like breast buds, which are firm mounds underneath the nipples that appear in early girl puberty—but they can also resemble more developed breasts. Either way, this can be the source of anxiety or shame, despite the fact that some studies estimate up to half of all teen boys have gynecomastia at some point.

Finally (because we're on paragraph eleven, after all!), a brief note about how testosterone levels fluctuate, not just at the start of adolescence but throughout the day and night, too. We have long known that humans have an internal circadian clock, but recent studies show that each of the organs inside our bodies has its own unique circadian rhythm. This means that they do their jobs or pump out their locally manufactured hormones according to their own central biological timekeeping device, with the liver on one schedule and the kidneys on another and the brain on yet another. The testicles are no exception, and so testosterone levels rise and fall during their own twenty-four-hour cycle, typically peaking in the morning hours. Organs also have lifetime clocks, and the testicles abide here, too. The lifetime peak of testosterone production occurs in males during their teens and early twenties—after that, the maximum amount of T pumped out by the testicles tends to be lower, which explains the onslaught of ads on TV marketing the hormone to older guys (*"Got low T . . . ?"*). While the circadian and lifetime rhythms of testosterone are clearly real, the normal range of testosterone in males is generally fairly wide and there is no standard definition of "low T." So this note is for you, dads: As is the case with every other ad pushing a medical product that your doctor doesn't necessarily think you need, be smart and remember that all bodies are different. Your perceived testosterone deficit may be a result of drawing your blood at a particular time of day, or comparing yourself to someone of a radically different age.

THE MALE MOOD SWING IS A THING

The sex hormones—namely estrogen and testosterone—affect the brain, a fact widely known for many decades. Generally speaking, estrogen gets credit for things like learning and memory while testosterone gets to claim sex drive. I'm drastically oversimplifying here, but my point is that hormones don't circulate solely below the neck; rather, they have profound effects on the way we think. Because hormone levels rise during puberty, it is fair to say that their impact on the brain rises too. This means that not only does testosterone captain the physical boy puberty ship, driving almost all of the body changes seen in adolescent guys short of hair growth and general greasiness, but it also impacts mood, behavior, and decision-making. None of this information is new.

Here's what may surprise you, because it sure has surprised scientists over the past few years: Testosterone directly impacts the way the male brain is organized. It binds to *neurons* (the workhorse cells in the brain) and rewires them by stimulating growth of their long arms (called *axons*), prompting these same axons to grow new connections with certain adjacent neurons while terminating connections with others. Testosterone also drives the production of *myelin*, the fatty cell layer that insulates neurons, making them far more efficient. This combination of effects means that the very presence of testosterone causes neurons to make new connections and then build the infrastructure necessary to speed up the flow of information along those paths—it literally hardwires the brain.

What's more, testosterone impacts certain parts of the brain with extra gusto. That's because these regions have more testosterone receptors, allowing them to better sense the presence of the hormone. The regions include the *amygdala,* generally considered the emotional epicenter of the brain; the *hippocampus,* which takes primary charge of memory; and the famous *prefrontal cortex,* known for planning, patience, and all-around emotional control.

I will tell you that during adolescence there isn't balance between the emotional part of the brain (which includes the amygdala and hippocampus) and the rational part (prefrontal cortex). Even though there are extra testosterone receptors in both places, the emotional areas mature faster, so they are able to send and receive messages more quickly. This helps to explain why your teenager might behave in unpredictable or even impulsive ways from time to time . . . or maybe it feels like all of the time. The hardwiring of the brain has everything to do with that, and it's covered in great detail in Chapter 5.

I bring this up now, though, because it's important to give testosterone a shout-out in the mood department. When it comes to tween and teen girl moods, pretty much everyone, regardless of whether or not they have a daughter, feels free to talk about swings and pin the blame on estrogen as girls ping-pong from high to low, happy to sad, silly to serious. It isn't just their new spectrum of emotional responses that gets our collective attention, but also the dramatic shift between one extreme and another. Well, testosterone causes its own swings, and now there's science to prove that the brain exhibits corresponding physical changes, too.

T is famous for triggering aggression and accompanying rage, but not everyone agrees that a direct line should be drawn here.* In fact, studies repeatedly demonstrate that testosterone has an equally large impact (if not greater, depending upon the data) on risk-taking and depression as well. These swings create a triangle of anger, impulsivity, and sadness. Think it's not fun for you as the parent? Try being the adolescent guy with all of that going on in his head.

CONNECTING T AND QUIET

The retreat of our boys is so common, it is almost a diagnostic symptom of adolescent maleness. Some parents really fight me on this, adamant that their boys still talk to them all the time, adding for extra measure, *We have a great relationship.* Congratulations! Not every kid experiences every symptom of puberty. But the vast majority of parents are grateful to read that their son isn't the only one retreating. If your guy is still super young, you will be glad to know this before one day in the near future when he basically shuts the door in your face. And even those who have chatty sons often look back, years later, and recognize that their talker talked a little bit less at some point during this stage.

Unfortunately, there exist no decent studies measuring the role of testosterone in the silence of the pubescent boy, a fact that drives me nuts given that this phenomenon seems to affect almost every boy I meet, at least to some degree.

Maybe the research hasn't been done because quietness isn't considered a masculine feature in the same way as body type or libido or fistfights. Those endpoints are certainly more measur-

---

* In *The Truth About Hormones*, Vivienne Parry describes a different path: higher levels of testosterone are correlated with popularity, which can certainly be tethered to risk-taking but not really to aggression. It's the deprivation of being low-status, not testosterone itself, she argues, that drives a kid to be violent. An interesting theory—I hope more research will follow here.

able, making for an easier study, not to mention that rage is a sexier headline than silence.

Or perhaps it's because boys seem to outgrow their quiet: grown men are usually not nearly as hushed as their teenage selves. Some are, but most of us interact with multisyllabic adult males all the time. If testosterone is the cause of pubescent quietness, then why do older guys who have just as much T on board—if not more—start talking again? And besides, if they generally outgrow the phenomenon, why make a big deal of it?

There is a logic to not talking about not talking, particularly when it's transient. Every adult male I have ever asked emphasized that this was a normal phase in his life, concluding there is nothing to be worried about. Focus on the overtly negative stuff, they say, like the testosterone-fueled rage that ends with fistfights or gun violence or sexual aggression. It's a hard sell to create a national conversation around half the population spending a few years not wanting to be part of the conversation.

Should we worry if the act of shutting out adults is normal and, in most cases, short-lived? Pediatricians and developmental psychologists are well aware of the switch that happens in both genders around the age of twelve, when suddenly kids care far more about the opinions of their peer group and far less about those of their parents. This change corresponds with changes in the brain, where specific areas within the limbic system (hello again, amygdala and hippocampus!) become more active when friends are nearby; interestingly, this is the case whether their presence is physical or virtual (hello, social media!). In other words, they're not quiet around their buddies. Perhaps the silence of our sons should be viewed as a temporary retreat from adults and caretakers and nothing more than that, especially because with their friends they are often fully animated, their brains literally lighting up.

———

The selective and transient nature of our boys' silence may ultimately explain why researchers haven't furiously worked to understand why it happens. Still, when they stop talking we often
do the same in return, and given the current culture, the consequences of parents not talking to their sons are growing increasingly severe. That's what this whole book is really about: if
we don't talk to our boys, often and intensely, about all of the
things covered in the chapters that follow—big-ticket subjects
like the escalating violence seen in easy-access online pornography and on school campuses—then we cannot help them prepare for the consequences, some of which are arguably far
greater today than they were a generation ago.

In order to be able to talk through all of these charged
topics—not just muster the courage to bring them up but actually get the conversations going—we must put a foot in the
ever-slamming door. We can respect our sons' need for privacy
(and testosterone's bodily impact gives them plenty of reasons
to crave privacy) while at the same time insisting on regular
check-ins about school, friends, feelings, frustrations, victories,
and failures. Because whether or not their quiet is a derivative
of changing levels of testosterone, if we fully accept our sons'
silence and don't insist on keeping a conversational thread alive,
trust me when I say we will face a much steeper climb when a
heavyweight topic rears its head.

There exists tons of research supporting the notion that talk
is healthy: when kids voice current concerns to supportive lis-
teners, they benefit from their community of advisors; when
they put words to future potential issues and think through how
they might react, they train their brains to respond more logically in the heat of the moment. Ultimately, talking about what's
going on in your life at any age, but especially during puberty,
keeps people safer and healthier. Talking is associated with a
stronger sense of self, as well as reduced risk-taking or more
forethought (or . . . wait for it . . . both!). Even when we don't

get in front of a situation with our kids, open lines of communication allow for conversation afterward.

Said another way, while not talking isn't necessarily a bad thing, talking *is* a good one.

I wish this chapter could draw a direct line between rising testosterone levels and the quiet we see in teenage boys, but I don't have that data. Regardless of why our boys go quiet, they do so at the same time that their bodies are pumping out higher doses of a hormone that clearly impacts their physiques, emotional states, and physical responses. Maybe one day T will be identified as the source of this stereotypical silence, maybe not. It might not matter. What does matter is recognizing the effect of not talking to our sons when they arguably need conversation the most.

HOW TO TALK TO BOYS ABOUT . . . TESTOSTERONE

1. IT'S NOT A BAD WORD. Neither are any of the body parts, their transformations, or their actions, by the way. The earlier we get into the habit of describing normal body functions, the more likely our sons (and daughters) are to use the right vocab when asking a question. This saves us tremendous confusion and miscommunication! So use biological words often, defining them when needed.

2. IT'S NOT A DRUG THEY SHOULD BE TAKING. That is, unless testosterone is prescribed by a doctor specifically for your son. Boys see testosterone advertised everywhere, promising bigger, better, more sexual bodies, so some think they need to take it. And like every other medication these days, there are ways to get some if you really want some. So talk to your son about staying away from hormone supplements unless there is a medical reason to use them.

3. IT'S A GREAT ENTRY INTO A BROADER CONVERSA-TION ABOUT BODY EXPECTATIONS. If you start paying a little more attention to the information floating around about T, you will quickly get a taste of what your son lives each day. Take the opportunity to say something when testosterone is mentioned in the context of manliness, machismo, or muscles. Frankly, take the opportunity even when testosterone isn't mentioned. Boys in the early stages of puberty have big expectations about what they will look like in the future. It's important to know what your son anticipates and then to help him manage that.

Chapter Three
YES, YOUR NINE-YEAR-OLD MIGHT BE IN PUBERTY

FOR JUST A MOMENT, TAKE A trip back in time to your nine-year-old self. I don't care if you are male or female, by the way. You just need to be older than nine.

You were probably in third or fourth grade. Maybe you had a group of friends, or maybe one bestie. You might flash back to a moment of newfound independence, like walking home alone from school or feeling the freedom of trick-or-treating without a parent right by your side. There were Saturday morning cartoons and school recess on the blacktop and, even if you didn't eat it, Wonder Bread was everywhere.

I am guessing you didn't flash back to the body changes of puberty. At nine, it was the rare girl who had to manage boobs or hair or curves. As for boys, forget about it—the start of looking manly was still years off.

Today, everything is different for our kids. Wonder Bread is bad for you. Halloween is fraught with toxic makeup and texting drivers who don't notice throngs of kids. Walking home alone from school, at least in many areas, is considered downright rebellious. Today a nine-year-old might be in third grade, but he might still be in second because so many kids start kindergarten at increasingly later ages. In another year, half of all his pals will have their own digital device—yes, that's right, the average age for a first phone or iPad or other mobile connected device considered "theirs" is now ten (and almost undoubtedly, by the time this book is published, that number will be lower). When we were nine, most of us remember trying to make a call in private by stretching the phone cord as far as it would go—hopefully into another room or even a closet, so that we could shut a door for privacy. Okay, so some of the younger parents reading this remember lugging bulky cordless phones into the other room. Doesn't really matter, because there was always another handset somewhere in the house, a perfect source of sibling torture as one kid could listen silently to another's conversation or, worse yet, interrupt with heavy breathing. There's no such thing as picking up another phone to listen in anymore, and there are barely any corded handsets in existence, let alone ones with cords long enough to wind around yourself.

All of which is to say that today's nine-year-olds live in a world that is so far beyond what we ever could have imagined when we were nine, it almost makes your brain ache. And now layer on this: many of them are in puberty. The downward age shift in body development among girls has been written about extensively. In fact, for a long while this was thought to *only* be a girl phenomenon. But boys, as it turns out, are in the exact same boat. Not all of them, but many. Most. Maybe your kid, even if you don't think so.

THE ACTUAL DEFINITION OF PUBERTY

Let's start with a refresher on what puberty actually is, because the word seems to have a highly flexible definition, even though it really doesn't. *Puberty* is the body and brain's path to sexual maturity and reproductive ability, encompassing every step necessary for a child to transform into a person capable of making offspring. As hard as it may be to comprehend, it's possible that your baby-faced, immature, not-a-hair-on-his-body little boy could be in it.

It helps to remember from just a few pages ago that at the very start of boy puberty, the brain tells the testicles to begin making testosterone, kicking off a feedback loop that stimulates the testicles (and penis) to grow. But S-L-O-W-L-Y. In fact, nothing about puberty is quick, no matter how suddenly it seems to sneak up on a kid. The body takes its sweet time ramping up testosterone production, not to mention growing and developing, which is precisely why boys don't exhibit the classically well-known testosterone effects—like bulking-up muscle mass and deepening of the voice—until long after this hormone's debut.

And remember that some younger guys might look a little more advanced thanks to the appearance of things like hair and acne, but these are pubertal red herrings . . . sort of. They're part of the general gist of puberty, but they don't signify maturation of the testicles; nor do they have anything to do with testosterone or the baby-making machinery. Instead, hair and grease and sweat emerge on their own independent timetable, thanks to androgens made in the adrenal glands. Which is ironic, because while armpit fuzz or zits or body odor are sometimes the very first pubescent changes parents will notice in their son, they aren't the changes that signify any sort of below-the-belt march toward manhood—it's just that most of the time the two hormone paths coincide.

The testicular ramp-up and distant testosterone effects are so slow that it is not uncommon for us parents (along with the rest of the outside world) to be left clueless about our son's foray into puberty for a year, even two. Most of what is happening is subtle and hidden. Some boys may notice for themselves when their testicles start to grow—if they are the noticing type, that is, and many are not—but the rest of us generally don't see a thing.

Which makes it slightly farcical that the testicles hang down outside of the body. Unlike girls' sex-hormone-producing ovaries, which are tucked away inside the abdomen, testicles are out there and we could actually see growth if we looked for it. But let's just say that checking out your kid's genitals isn't widely socially acceptable. This cultural pattern is reinforced by the fact that just as puberty begins to kick in, boys typically become extremely private, covering up and changing behind closed doors. Don't even try talking to your tween or teenage son when he's taking a shower. There are pros and cons to this belief that we shouldn't look down there, and certainly there are cultures around the globe that don't share it. (Just as certainly, there are American boys who feel uber-comfortable parading around their homes bottomless, so they don't share it, either.) Perhaps those parents who do have eyes on their kids' genitals also know precisely when their boys are about to experience a rapid growth spurt, drop an octave, and adopt monosyllabic answers to deeply probing questions.

Still, it makes sense to me why, as a society, we have landed where we have: at least outside the home, private parts are private. This social norm begins with a pattern of recognizing that your body is yours and you should have dominion over it. Future sexual partners—even just future admirers—are expected to ask before looking or touching. This system has its own glaring flaws (for instance, some forms of sexual expression can be met with shame), but it provides a rationale at least for why we don't all just walk down the street in the buff. Long way of saying: it's the rare parent who tells me they know what's happening to their son's genitals . . . and therefore most parents are utterly unaware of when their boys enter puberty.

If the only way to know when our sons are in the early stages of puberty is to check whether their testicles are growing, it seems a little less egregious that girls have been the focus of most of the attention on this topic: early girl changes like breast buds and widening hips are far more public, with or without clothes on.

THE HISTORY OF EARLY PUBERTY STARTED WITH GIRLS

The visibility of girl puberty plays a significant role in why we have come to accept that our girls, but not our boys, enter this process sooner than they used to. This divergent story dates back to 1997, when Marcia Herman-Giddens, a clinician and researcher at Duke University Medical Center, published a study of more than 17,000 girls showing that they were starting to develop at increasingly younger ages. Before Herman-Giddens, the last—and first—time that puberty was studied on a large scale occurred back in the late 1940s in Britain, when a pediatrician named James Tanner and his associate Reginald Whitehouse began what would become a decades-long survey of human development. They photographed children multiple times per year, documenting the transformation of their breasts and genitals. Nothing of the sort had ever been done (and certainly couldn't be done today!), but thanks to the information collected, Tanner and Whitehouse were able to quantify the stages of puberty. Still to this day, doctors all over the world refer to the five Tanner stages when they describe the progression of any particular child's pubertal development. And until 1997, most physicians used Tanner's data to advise parents when to expect puberty to begin: according to Tanner, the average girl entered puberty just after her eleventh birthday and the average boy started at around 11.5 years.

One thing Tanner and Whitehouse did quite well was to study their subjects on multiple occasions over many years, measuring the progress of any given child over time. This study design, called a *longitudinal study*, leads to very different—arguably better—results compared with a *cross-sectional study* that may measure a large group of kids of different ages but only looks at each child once. While longitudinal studies often provide richer data, they also take more time and therefore cost more money, explaining why most of the puberty studies that followed Tanner's have been cross-sectional instead.

Even though Tanner and Whitehouse's study design was outstanding, it had one major flaw: they only used photographs. In fact, neither Tanner nor Whitehouse physically examined the kids. Laying hands on a patient is far more accurate than looking at a picture, and so their data has been questioned by many. But over the years, as researchers have tried to confirm or reject Tanner's original results by using inarguably better methods, they have all done it slightly differently—some have examined the kids, some have not; some have looked at kids in different age ranges; some have used a variety of physical and hormonal markers, many of which were not even available when Tanner was working; and some have even come up with their own definition of what it means to "start puberty." All of this has made it nearly impossible to compare and contrast the newer data with Tanner's original results. Frankly, it has been tricky even to agree on general trends.*

Nonetheless, Tanner's declaration of when puberty "should" begin for both boys and girls remained the gold standard until Herman-Giddens came along.

Marcia Herman-Giddens wasn't looking to be a disruptor. But she spent her days examining children and couldn't help noticing that their development was beginning significantly

---

* One major piece of data that came out of Tanner's study was that it typically took a little more than two years from the beginning of girl puberty (breast budding, in his study) to getting a period. This set many standards, including the idea of a "normal" interval between starting puberty and reaching a major landmark of the process. But this milestone of pubertal progression was—and remains—exclusively female. There is no period parallel in the male experience . . . making boy puberty even trickier to quantify. And, as you are about to read, that timeline for girls from breast buds to bleeding has also changed.

sooner than Tanner predicted, particularly among girls. She wanted to figure out if her population of girls was advancing through puberty prematurely or if girls across the United States were experiencing this same shift. Were her patients outliers? Or was she witnessing a new normal? Herman-Giddens partnered with the American Academy of Pediatrics and a network of doctors across the country to examine, measure, and document the pubertal growth and development of their patients. The data ultimately confirmed her own experience in the clinic: girls were entering puberty up to one and a half years earlier than Tanner predicted. It turned out that the age of entry depended upon ethnicity, with black girls starting to develop youngest, followed by Hispanic girls, and then white girls.* It's worth noting that the age a girl first got her period hadn't budged nearly as much, arriving only three to six months sooner than Tanner had reported decades earlier. In other words, Herman-Giddens stumbled onto the fact that while puberty—at least in girls—seemed to be starting younger, it wasn't progressing any faster. This phase of life, one that anecdotally neither girls nor their parents particularly relish, was actually lengthening.

Herman-Giddens's work took the world by storm. Headlines about her findings dominated newspapers and magazines. Despite the lack of online viral spread—this was years before the establishment of news feeds and social media—the attention was enormous. And it still is: over the past two decades, Herman-Giddens has been hailed by many for quantifying a phenome-

---

* The fact that only white, Hispanic, and black girls were studied is not lost on me. There are many other ethnicities, not to mention multiracial kids, who aren't represented here. Data about these girls—and in later studies, boys— have been omitted because over the years the studies haven't included large enough sample sizes for these populations. But hopefully this issue is on its way to correction. Certainly there's an effort to fix the lack of info about Asian Americans, with small studies appearing over the past few years. These show that Asian American girls tend to develop around the same time or even later than white girls.

non that parents and doctors could see in their homes and offices. She did, indeed, call out a new normal.*

The summer Herman-Giddens's paper debuted, I began my pediatrics training, working alongside a fellow resident named Louise Greenspan. Years later, long after we shared all-night shifts in the hospital, Louise would go on to become a pediatric endocrinologist and lead the studies that looked to prove—or disprove—Herman-Giddens's research. Starting in 2005, Greenspan in San Francisco along with researchers in Cincinnati and New York measured the pubertal trajectory of 1,200 girls. By 2010, they made their own headlines when they showed that not only was Herman-Giddens right, but in the intervening decade the starting age for girl puberty had crept down even younger. Take breast development: by age eight, just under half of all black girls in their study had begun to develop breasts; almost one in three Hispanic girls and one in six white girls too. Breast buds were not uncommon even as young as seven, occurring in nearly 23% of black girls, 15% of Hispanic girls, and 10% of white girls in her study. Those are first- and second-graders.

Girl puberty was rapidly becoming a popular field of study, not to mention a headline grabber. What amazed me most with all of this emerging data was that boys were entirely left out. I remember thinking way back in 1997 that the absence of the boy conversation was odd. Clearly, boys go through puberty too (said every parent everywhere who has been in a car with a pu-

---

*   That said, she has been criticized by others who suggest her study population was not representative of the greater U.S. girl population, and that her methods of assessment weren't ideal. To the latter point: Herman-Giddens started her study when the youngest girls were just three years old, critical because her goal was to catch as many girls as possible before their entrée into puberty. She ended the age of enrollment when the girls reached twelve, which is well before the completion of puberty—and even before a first period—for the vast majority. So while her study group did not allow her to follow through the full progression of puberty, it did allow Herman-Giddens to measure the front end of this stage of physical development.

bescent boy at the end of a long, sweaty day). But there was absolutely no urgency, not even interest really, around the question of pubertal timing among guys—the buzz was about girls, and so were the vast majority of the studies. In fact, boys were almost entirely sidelined until Herman-Giddens herself sought to remedy the oversight. In 2012 she published what should have been another bombshell set of results, this time about boys. Amazingly, they fizzled.

OH NO HE ISN'T! WHY MOST OF US MISS THE START OF BOY PUBERTY

When I give talks and present findings about earlier boy development, I watch as parents shake their heads and sometimes even mumble a version of: *Oh no, no, no, lady. Not my son, no way!* In fact, the topic of when your son will (or did) start puberty is the one where I get the most pushback from parents. Not immunizations, not screen-time rules. It's when I suggest that their little boys may actually be men-in-the-making that parents freak.* And that's why I shouldn't be surprised, at least in hindsight, about the reception of Herman-Giddens's boy data.

I feel for you, fellow parents who are sure your boy isn't developing yet, because I have a son. And, for what it's worth, a daughter—a built-in basis of comparison. It makes sense that we notice girl puberty, because we cannot deny when a little girl

---

* One reason why parents push back so hard when I talk about earlier puberty is that they fear the hormonal onslaught of this stage. From a cultural health standpoint, we have been trained to think that hormones are bad, and that exposure to them causes all sorts of future ailments. Breast cancer! Autoimmune disease! Depression! And yes, in fact, reproductive hormones like our favorite villainess estrogen have been linked with a long list of medical issues. But they are also critical to physical development and health maintenance, and *not* having hormones floating around your bloodstream can be as problematic as having too many or having the wrong ones.

suddenly develops the external features of womanhood. Trust me, I tried. Even though we all do our best not to notice (because it feels wrong to notice, right?!), we see the transformation. At least parents do; and by the way, it's not at all wrong to notice how your own child is growing and developing. With girls morphing before our eyes, though, it's easy to miss our boys' puberty in its earliest stage.

That's because not only do pubescent boys *not* become curvaceous, but most of them don't really change at all for the first year or two—they still look and act like little boys. Their early puberty is essentially invisible to the outside world because the only measurable changes are happening inside their testicles. And we've already walked through the reasons why any change that is limited to the area under the underpants is easy to miss.

That said, there is one group that's supposed to look at the entire body, including down there: pediatricians. And they even have a tool at their disposal to measure testicular size, so that they can actually get an accurate gauge of growth. It's called an *orchidometer* and it looks like a necklace of a dozen beads, each slightly larger than the last. The smallest beads represent prepubescent testes (they range from 1 to 3 milliliters or approximately ¼–½ teaspoon, because testicles are measured in volume); the biggest beads represent fully developed testes (anywhere from 15 to 25 milliliters or 3 to 5 teaspoons). You can only imagine the look on boys' faces when they learn what this necklace is. Many of them laugh, but not all! Unfortunately, some pediatricians don't even look at the genitals. Most do, but many of them won't always explain what they are seeing. And even if they describe it to the boys, it's not like the majority of guys run home and report that part of the checkup; so unless a parent is present for the conversation, they won't hear the news. In the end, often the pediatrician is the only one left knowing which boys are in puberty. Everyone else is just pretty much standing around in the dark.

In 2012, Herman-Giddens aimed to do for boy puberty what

she had done for girl puberty, mostly because she was seeing a similar trend and no one seemed to be paying any attention to it. Using the same network of doctors as in the girl study, she looked at data from more than 4,000 boys, each one examined by a health care professional. This included measuring their testicular size. In the end, Herman-Giddens found that boys, too, were developing earlier—anywhere from a year and a half to two years sooner than Tanner predicted. Remember how Tanner had said boys enter puberty, on average, around 11.5 years of age? Now white boys were beginning to develop just after their tenth birthday, black boys shortly after they turned nine, and Hispanic boys somewhere in between.

By looking under boys' underpants and measuring their testicles, Herman-Giddens finally shined a light—literally—on information that was overlooked and undiscussed by pretty much everyone, from parents to researchers, even to many doctors.

This is not to say that boys weren't studied at all between Tanner in the 1940s, '50s, and '60s and Herman-Giddens in 2012. They were. There is a massive ongoing study called NHANES (short for National Health and Nutrition Examination Survey, which in its prior iteration was called the National Health Examination Survey, or NHES), run out of the Centers for Disease Control and Prevention since 1959. Amazingly, data back to the 1980s and '90s show earlier onset of male puberty, compared with the timing predicted by Tanner. Other studies around the turn of the millennium also documented what Herman-Giddens later showed: boy puberty was beginning sooner than Tanner said it should. But ultimately all of this boy data was criticized because the studies weren't perfect—the sample size was too small, or wasn't representative of the greater U.S. population, or the methods were flawed. It took until Herman-Giddens came along, again, for this topic to gain traction. And *still* no one seemed to care. Boys and their earlier puberty never made headlines, not even when everyone was freaking out about girl development, and not even when the headline-making scientist herself tried to draw attention to them.

WHY BOY PUBERTY HEADLINES FIZZLED

Some people think that I believe the Internet and its accompanying screens are entirely negative, because as a pediatrician I talk a lot about how screens rob kids of sleep, and how they curate content that many kids aren't ready for. But technology is not my enemy—it is a friend I embrace every day. And on one particular day, I used it to reach out to Herman-Giddens. I looked up one of her articles, clicked on her name in the byline, and landed on a biography page that included her email address. I sent off a note, and amazingly Herman-Giddens replied within minutes. Before I knew it, we were chatting on the phone. See? I still love screens and the Internet, even though they are sometimes the bane of my parenting existence.

I wanted to understand why boys had been left out of the conversation for so long. Why has there been so much less interest in studying boys than girls? And once studies on boys *were* done, why did the results fall so flat compared with the hoopla around the girl data?

"The reaction was exactly what I expected . . . exactly," Herman-Giddens told me. "Unfortunately, there's a titillating interest in the budding sexuality of young girls. Like the Lolita syndrome sort of thing or whatever you want to call it. Unfortunately, it's there. And in my opinion, that's the big reason. Plus, the fact that girls can get pregnant and are more likely to be victimized than boys. I think a lot of [the focus on girl puberty] is the prurient interest in young girls' sexuality.

"Obviously girl puberty is visible to everyone—it's very public," she continued, confirming my own theories on the topic. "Everyone can see the breasts developing. And menses is public, at least within the family. You can't miss it. Whereas in boys, the first sign of puberty—they don't even know themselves, probably. The testes start to enlarge and it's very subtle. The parents certainly don't see it."

Herman-Giddens and I agree: blossoming girls are seen—for better or for worse. Blossoming boys aren't. It's simply a visibility issue, intimately connected to the nature of how boys versus girls actually begin to blossom.

Beyond the when, there's the *why* of the changes themselves. What underlies this recent acceleration of the start of pubertal development in the first place? I wish I could give you a simple, straightforward answer, but no one really knows just yet. After Louise Greenspan published her girl puberty data, she authored a book called *The New Puberty* aiming to explain just that. There are researchers working tirelessly to figure out if there is something in our world that can explain why, on average, our kids are beginning to develop younger than we ever did. I am not one of these scientists, but in my estimation, after having read every book and article I could get my hands on over the past several years, the cause will turn out to be not one thing but many. We will, in the end, have a long laundry list of things that we put into and onto our bodies, purposefully or inadvertently, which ultimately activate the puberty machinery earlier. To date, there is good evidence that excess weight does it, as do chemicals that impersonate estrogen. But no one has come up with a unifying culprit, let alone an *Eat This, Not That!* list to keep kids from developing at increasingly younger ages. I am beginning to feel certain that the answer will never be that simple.

I do take solace, though, in some advice passed along to me by Greenspan: "There has to be a bottom," she told me, "and I think we are pretty close to it." In other words, no, our kids' kids won't be pubescent kindergarteners.

So yes, your nine-year-old might be in puberty. Herman-Giddens collected her boy data between 2005 and 2010, measuring testicular growth as the best first sign of having crossed the puberty threshold. Out of 100 white nine-year-olds, 26 qualified as pubescent; for black boys, the number was 43, and for Hispanics, 44. By age ten, these numbers jumped to 44% for white boys, 49% for Hispanic boys, and a whopping 72% for black boys. Unfortunately, all bets are off for unstudied ethnicities like Asians and kids of multiracial heritage. Bear in mind, this data is scientifically old, much of it having been collected well over a decade ago. To put that time frame into context, the youngest child at the start of Herman-Giddens's study is now able to drink alcohol legally. So if this is the new normal, perhaps the needle has continued to move over the past decade-plus.

I know all too well the desire to see our sons as little boys for as long as possible. And in so many ways, they are. Just because they have testosterone on board doesn't mean that they will suddenly make mature decisions—oftentimes it's quite the opposite! So in the end, perhaps the best thing we can do as parents is to open ourselves to the facts but contextualize them, reframing what they do and don't mean. Yes, your nine-year-old might be in puberty. No, you don't have to examine his body to confirm whether this is the case. But use this information to change how you talk to him about physical and emotional shifts that occur thanks to surging testosterone. You think you are freaked out by the fact that he might have bigger genitals or hair down there? As I said earlier in this book and will say again: Imagine what's going through *his* mind. Then start to talk about it. Normalize it. However you approach the conversation, let him know that, while you respect his privacy, you also are here to answer questions, talk through new facts, or even just listen. Puberty brings with it a whole host of potential body insecurities, from acne to stench to wet dreams to voice cracks. Pretending like none of it is happening only magnifies the insecurity.

If you are absolutely certain that your son is not in puberty, that I have all of this wrong because you have a late bloomer who you know, for a fact, still has testicles on the small side of the orchidometer strand, then read on. Because just as important as acknowledging that many boys are developmentally ahead of where nine- and ten- and eleven-year-olds were a generation ago, some are lagging behind their peers. And this lack of development carries its own significant burdens.

HOW TO TALK TO BOYS ABOUT . . . EARLIER PUBERTY

1. BE THE SOURCE. Of information, that is. Let your son know that he can come to you with questions, and give him some introductory facts even when he doesn't ask. This does not need to be complicated! Starting with basics like *Hey, did you know that if you don't use soap and really lather when you are in the shower, you won't smell clean?* can be a social-life saver.

2. DON'T INSIST ON COLLECTING DATA YOURSELF. If you're not sure whether your son is in puberty and you are dying to know, don't be the parent who examines their own kid. Take this from me—a pediatrician— even I didn't do that. Many boys begin to seek privacy as their bodies start to change. Respecting their modesty is more important than knowing whether or not their testicles have grown. If you really need to know, make an appointment with your pediatrician.

3. THIS IS GOING TO TAKE A LONG TIME, SO PACE YOURSELF. Puberty may be starting earlier these days, but it's not moving any faster. If anything, it has slowed down. So you have lots of time to start big conversations with questions like *Has anyone explained to you what a hormone is?*

Chapter Four
LATER, DUDE

TECHNICALLY SPEAKING, A LATE BLOOMER IS any boy who hasn't entered puberty (translation: his testicles haven't started to grow) by the time he is fourteen. And here's the thing about being a late-blooming boy: it's almost always a double whammy. Not only are these guys slow to develop in that puberty kind of way—they've got no zits, no bulging muscles, and their high-pitched voices haven't begun to drop or even crack—but they are also generally not growing taller at the same crazy pace as their peers. Some will still sprout small patches of pubic or underarm hair, and others might give off a whiff of that pubescent B.O., because these are features ruled by the adrenal androgens rather than testosterone (go back two chapters if that's confusing). By and large, though, late bloomers start high school looking a lot like the little boys they were when they started middle school, while everyone else has morphed . . . some of them years ago.

Men who have emerged out the other side of a very delayed start to puberty have become increasingly open on the subject. In casual conversations, interviews, essays, blog posts, novels, screenplays, and anywhere else one finds a voice today, many of these guys describe what it was like to be treated as children when really they were on the cusp of adulthood, some even chronologically *in* adulthood. Their stories of steep social and emotional tolls are often told with humor—except that painful kind of humor which makes the listener wince while laughing. And while many of them point out a silver lining—like the athletes, scrappy fighters who worked harder than their bigger, stronger teammates and swear by this as the key to their success not just on the field or court but in life—I have yet to come across a man who bloomed late as a boy and loved it.

No matter how isolating the experience feels—and it can seem painfully lonely—it's a statistical fact that 2.5 out of every 100 boys is a late bloomer. Well, kind of. Since the timing of puberty is currently in flux anyhow, with a slow downward start-time slide, today's "late" can appear more exaggerated than ever. And at the tail end of the development curve, some are destined to be even later than others.

This chapter is about the boys who represent the last of the last: by the time they look down and see signs of sexual maturity, every girl and almost every other boy in school has been there, done that. In a world of growing up faster and faster, they aren't. It can be hard to imagine longing for acne or that awkward in-between 'stache, especially as a parent looking back through time. But everything in life is relative, and puberty straddles a boy's social world, his emotional health, and sometimes medical concerns all at the same time.

For late-blooming boys, the longer they go without the physical signs of adulthood, the further askew they may feel during a time in life that is already famously off-balance to begin with.

THE MEANING OF "LATE"

A quick crash course in statistics for those of you who need one (it will only last three paragraphs, I promise). The *mean* is the average. So if you want to know the average age of the onset of male puberty, you can ask a group of men (or even boys) how old they were when their puberty began and then take all of those ages, add them up, and divide by the number of people you asked. Of course, if you've read Chapter 3, you will know that most guys actually have no clue when they entered puberty, making for a difficult study. But still, researchers have tried. They have also asked parents, a group generally even more clueless about boy development than the boys themselves, given that the vast majority haven't seen their sons naked since sometime around the fourth or fifth grade. Pediatricians and health care professionals are the ones who can best speak to the start of puberty, because they examine kids and can see when boys' testicles begin to grow—they tell researchers that these days the average age a boy enters puberty is nine if he's black and ten if he's Hispanic or white. The jury's still out on timing for Asian and multiracial boys, but once those studies are (finally!) done they will almost certainly fall somewhere within the same range.

Beyond the mean, there's the *standard deviation from the mean*. A standard deviation is a measure of how spread-out the numbers are within a data set. When research results are graphed, they often look like a bell-shaped curve. A line can be drawn straight down from the bell's apex, bisecting the bell and visually representing the mean. A narrow data range makes a tall and skinny bell, while a broad data range looks like a lower, flatter bell. That tall, skinny bell has a small standard deviation, with most of the results clustering around a central average (they don't deviate much); the wide, flat bell has a large standard deviation, with results varying widely from the mean (a good number of the data points are, basically, deviants). Now let's tell the story of boy puberty using this graph. The average start age of, say, ten for white boys doesn't tell us anything about how widely the start time for development varies: based on just the mean, we have no clue how old the very oldest or young the very youngest pubescent boys might be. It would be one thing if I told you that the youngest boy to enter puberty is nine and the oldest is eleven, with an average age of ten (a super narrow bell); it would be a completely different curve if I said the youngest is three and the oldest seventeen, with the same average of ten (a bell so low and long, it might look more like a hump). In other words, the mean is important but the standard deviation from the mean tells the story of the bigger group's experience. By the way, neither of these ranges reflects reality—the truth is somewhere in between.

Last statistical fact for now: by definition, approximately 68% of all results fall within one standard deviation on either side of the mean, and 95% fall within two standard deviations. That leaves 5% of the results falling outside of two standard deviations—the two tails of the statistical bell curve—with half (2.5%) above and half (the other 2.5%) below. And it's the 2.5% on either end that stand out as the exceptions. This is an important fact, the basis for so much of the research we all hear bandied about in news stories and casual conversation. Most studies aim to identify a typical path (the *norm*) within two standard deviations from the mean, whether a researcher is looking at weight, IQ, shoe size, income, home price, screen time, happiness, life span . . . Pretty much every metric in our world has an average and a standard deviation. Each one has a set of outliers too, generally defined as the top and bottom 2.5%.

This explains why 2.5 out of every 100 boys is a late bloomer. It's simply a statistical definition. Ninety-five percent of all boys develop within a specific age range deemed "normal," with 2.5% early and 2.5% late. Here's the catch: if you learned anything from Chapter 3, it's that when it comes to puberty, the definition of normal is changing, and the average start time is moving younger and younger. This means that late bloomers should be blooming younger too. Either that or the standard deviation from the mean is getting bigger, and the late bloomers are blooming even later relative to their average counterparts. No surprise here: once again the data is lacking. That's why, for the purposes of this chapter, we are stuck with an older definition of what it means to bloom late; and it's also why I used the caveat "kind of" at the start. Right now, any boy whose testicles haven't begun to grow by age fourteen is considered a late bloomer. That means his physical development lags four or five years behind average boys his own age, depending upon race—but practically speaking he might be as many as six or seven years behind the earliest guys to mature. When you're only fourteen, a gap of six or seven years is gargantuan!

All this number crunching is meant to clarify the following simple point: even though a late-blooming boy may feel like the last to mature—and very alone in this particular boat—he's not. There's a group of guys in the trenches with him, about 50,000 boys out of the two million born every year in the United States, as a matter of fact (or math), who are late as well. So, no matter how alienating the experience may feel, late blooming isn't rare—it happens in one out of forty boys, which is, medically speaking, pretty frequent. It just doesn't necessarily *feel* so common, especially for the latest of the late.

There is a long laundry list of reasons why some boys (and girls, too) don't tip into puberty on time, but by far the most common is something called *constitutional delay*. Basically, it's the medical term for late puberty that happens for no obvious reason but sorts itself out by age eighteen without any medical intervention. Well over half of all late bloomers are eventually diagnosed with constitutional delay (some studies put it as high as 75%), and in approximately two-thirds of these cases one or both parents also had constitutional delay—either the mom got her period for the first time after age fourteen, or the dad's growth spurt started after sixteen—making the explanation inarguably genetic. Constitutional delay is a diagnosis of exclusion, meaning that everything else that could cause the delay has been ruled out. So, to determine whether or not there's a medical issue at play, almost all of these boys wind up poked, prodded, and subjected to a number of tests. If after a series of blood draws and imaging studies everything looks normal, then there's "nothing wrong." (There may be nothing wrong medically, but these boys still look years younger than their friends and class-mates, sometimes well past high school graduation, which to them doesn't feel at all right. More on this in a moment.)

It is, for obvious reasons, even rougher when a medical expla-nation underlies the pubertal delay. Late blooming has a long list of medical causes, including a whole host of chronic illnesses like diabetes, inflammatory bowel disease, sickle cell anemia, and cystic fibrosis. Nutritional status plays a big role in puberty timing too, because if the body doesn't have enough energy re-serve to mature and do the things it needs to do once mature, it will slow its own progression. We think of this largely with re-spect to girls who may not have enough body fat to support a pregnancy and therefore don't get a regular period, but the same principle applies to boys who are malnourished or eating disor-dered, and even to some elite athletes with super-low body fat. Carrying a pregnancy is not the issue, because boys aren't plumbed to do that, but the body can slow down its development nonetheless. Another cause of delayed puberty is anything that messes with the production of sex hormones, which explains why tumors and testicular injuries wind up on the list, as well as conditions that interfere with the body's ability to produce cer-tain hormones in the first place. One very specific diagnosis that shows up in all the articles on this topic is Kallmann syndrome, which involves hormone deficiency and a poor sense of smell, but this only happens to one in 30,000 boys—so it's as low on the list of causes as it is popular to talk about. The most com-mon reason for delayed puberty is really no reason at all.

THE DOUBLE WHAMMY OF BLOOMING LATE

Here's how things go for many of the boys in this boat: around fourth or fifth grade, the girls begin to develop (not all of them, but many); and then, maybe it's around the end of fifth grade, there's that one guy who suddenly looks older. The rest of the boys in the class may or may not have noticed the girls evolving, but they almost certainly take note when the first fellow boy appears manly from out of nowhere. Sixth and seventh grades are a mishmash of heights, weights, and lip fuzz. There are guys with hairy armpits and nothing else, and others with acne that seems to appear in crops. Height can vary by a foot and a half between the shortest and the tallest boys in a class. Everyone—parents, doctors, even the boys themselves—accepts the wide range of variability, because the utter lack of any norm takes on its own sense of normalcy. But by eighth grade, when most kids are turning fourteen, suddenly everyone seems to have something adolescent going on—except for a dwindling group left behind in the dust.

Now I'm going to say it again, because it bears repeating over and over: the start of puberty is marked by testicular growth, not muscle growth or mustache growth or foot growth. It's testicular growth that results in testosterone production, which eventually triggers the appearance of secondary sex characteristics. But this can take a long time. If we were to examine the testicles of all the boys in an eighth-grade class, the vast majority would have started growing already. Even among the group that looks noticeably younger, most of them would have evidence of testicular action. But we don't pull their pants down and look—for good reason—and since it can take a couple of years for rising testosterone levels to show on the outside in any obvious way, this explains why the cluster of fourteen-year-old boys in a given class who look like they aren't in puberty yet tends to be a lot bigger than 2.5%. If I have just described your son, who looks like he's lagging in development but you have no clue what's happening under his underpants, make an appointment with your pediatrician before mentally lumping him into the group of true late bloomers. Technically, if his testicles measure 3 milliliters or more, he's not late. (That measurement and the tool used to collect it are covered in Chapter 3.)

The double whammy of late-onset puberty is that beyond

having to contend with looking young in the face (literally no facial hair, no pimples, still those cute baby cheeks), almost all of these boys are on the shorter side. Here's why: Part of puberty is the pubertal growth spurt. Kids grow an average of two inches per year, every year, between toddlerhood and puberty. But when they enter their growth spurt, they take off. Rapidly growing girls tend to gain around three inches a year for two to three years before they slow down dramatically; boys can grow four inches a year, sometimes more, which over a three-year span gives them an extra foot of height. So when a boy enters puberty on the early side, he will likely have his growth spurt earlier too. This means that he will not only look older, thanks to testosterone actions all over his body; he will also stand a whole lot taller, adding to the illusion of maturity.

Now, logic would say that, since part of puberty is a pubertal growth spurt, boys who are late bloomers will of course appear shorter than their friends during the years when they aren't in puberty, but they will catch up down the road when they have their own growth spurt. In fact, there's an argument to be made that late bloomers may even wind up taller than the rest, because they continue to grow for longer. This happens often among girls—the ones who develop youngest and get their periods first are also typically the tallest in the class until the end of middle school; but by late high school they wind up short by comparison because their friends who developed later just keep on growing and growing.

Turns out, the logic of growing later and growing more doesn't really apply to boys. Sure, there are stories of some guys who defy this, who grow slowly and steadily until they tip into late puberty, at which point they grow quickly and steadily and wind up overtaking their friends. But for the most part, later-blooming boys spend a chunk of their adolescence short for their age, and by the time they reach adulthood are no taller than their peers. Many are actually shorter. Why? Because a sizable number of late-blooming boys experience slower growth in those years when their bodies are refusing to enter puberty. Most kids grow about two inches per year every year before heading into their growth spurt, but these boys can slow down to an inch or even half an inch per year before they pick up again. That means their net height gain is less, and they wind up anywhere between one and a half and four inches shorter than their expected height. Maybe "triple whammy" is a better descriptor, because not only do late bloomers look younger and grow later, but many don't grow as much as boys who go through puberty on time.

Twenty years ago, Howard Kulin, chief of pediatric endocrinology at the Penn State College of Medicine, wrote this: "It is my impression that a good deal of statuary limitation can be sustained by patients who have some degree of sexual maturity. . . . Not to discount the trauma of reduced adult height in our society, but for children of pubertal age, their concern is how the outside world categorizes them with respect to peers." Kulin was way ahead of his time, and completely right, if you ask me. Boys who are shorter but progress through puberty on a typical time course seem to be less bothered by the fact of their relative shortness. Many don't like it, complain about it, want to fix it even, but it's a single hurdle and therefore feels more manageable if not surmountable. I haven't seen a study comparing shorter-but-maturing boys with shorter-and-not-maturing boys. That said, the boys who live through part (or all) of their teens with little or no outward signs of maturation have been studied quite a bit, and they are more likely than on-time and early bloomers to have one or more of the issues on the following laundry list: depression; low self-esteem; poor school performance; aggression toward peers or oppositional behavior toward adults; less contact with peers; and general immaturity, both socially and in terms of future goals. In other words, no one discounts the social and emotional impact of short stature in our society, but the impact of being a late bloomer seems bigger. Meaning worse.

TAKING ACTION WHEN HORMONES ARE INACTIVE

It feels downright wrong that one out of every forty guys goes through at least part of teenage life feeling utterly left behind and the medical response is: *Don't worry, we ruled out the bad stuff and it should all resolve on its own by eighteen. If it doesn't, we'll deal with things then.* Kulin's paper was a call to action, a refusal to accept this as the standard of care, because the social and emotional costs are too high. While I am not one to ever advocate overly aggressive medical intervention, especially for an issue that will likely resolve on its own, I think in this case we need to weigh the medical issues against the psychological ones. It's not fair to ask a boy to wait until he is eighteen in order to see if his testicles are going to start growing on their own, all the while ignoring the torment he feels because he's a high schooler who looks, for all intents and purposes, like he's a tween. I am not alone in this belief—many pediatricians and pediatric endo-crinologists (pediatricians specializing in hormones) feel the same way, and they don't just sit back, watchfully waiting until a boy has graduated from high school. They strike the delicate bal-ance of investigation without overmedicalization.

Meanwhile, parents too must advocate for their late-blooming boys, and the only way to do this effectively is to talk to them. If every single chapter in this book seems to land in the same place, that's no accident. The very first intervention for almost every boy puberty–related issue is conversation. When it comes to the timing of puberty, open up lines of communication with your son by asking him how he feels about his size or his moods or just the general fact of being late to the puberty party. Some boys are remarkably unfazed by any of it—they have a strong inherent sense of self, and feel like puberty will happen when it happens. These boys tend to look on the bright side, some re-lieved that they don't yet need to deal with the likes of skin breakouts and body reek. But most late-blooming boys, when asked (though sometimes not until the fourth, fifth, or even tenth go-around), will disclose feelings of frustration or sadness or worry. Like other boys their age, many retreat into quiet—the testicles don't have to start growing for our boys to start closing their doors—and they just need a little prodding in order to open up. So, work to talk through this silence, even (and maybe especially) with a boy who is not yet in the throes of puberty.

It's worth adding here that our questions can become leading: if we ask our sons how they feel about their development frequently enough, we may inadvertently plant seeds of worry—a classic backfire situation. So how do we encourage our boys, particularly the later bloomers, to talk about their feelings without accidentally causing a worry that wasn't there before? In much the same way that we manage all anticipatory guidance: we push where we think we need to push, share what we think we need to share, and generally make it up as we go along, getting most of it right and failing wildly in at least one area. If your son is particularly anxious, you will naturally frame your questions differently, because you've had his entire prepubescent lifetime to learn how to ask him sensitive questions. But even if he's stoic, be cautious about how you approach. Late blooming can be a particularly raw subject, and it's the quietest boys who will often further submerge their sadness or frustration, fooling us into the belief that they're okay.

Beyond talking, address the physiological facts. If your son doesn't show signs of puberty by the time he is fourteen, take him to the pediatrician so he can be evaluated. In many cases, a quick testicular exam will reveal that he actually *is* in puberty; he's just slightly later than many of his friends and it will take time for the testosterone he's making to show itself externally. The relief for those boys is palpable—even for the ones who never made a peep about being concerned. For others, there's no testicular growth, and this warrants the beginning of an evaluation. Remember that as many as three-quarters of all late bloomers have constitutional delay, so every test and study will come back normal. But that leaves one-quarter who have something underlying their delayed puberty, and that something may need treatment.

A note about what to say before you have your son evaluated, because a trip to the doctor can be anxiety-provoking for some kids: approach it like you would anything else—an earache, weird rash, random bulge where the belly button used to be—and reassure your son that you just want to have him checked head-to-toe, but you're not worried. Need an excuse to get him to a regular annual checkup? Puberty is a great one!

Having social and emotional help in place makes a tremendous difference to boys, especially since the long list of issues associated with late puberty includes things like depression, aggression, and social isolation. Therapists, school counselors, and other trusted adults provide invaluable support here. If you can, find someone who himself went through puberty late—there's nothing like a confidant who's lived it.

And then there's medication. Pediatricians and pediatric endocrinologists have the ability to prescribe androgens—like the hormone testosterone—to see if they can tip a teenager into puberty when his body won't do it on its own. There are pros and cons to treating late puberty with medicines, though. While boys given androgens may begin sexual maturation, start growing more rapidly, and as a result report better mood, stronger social ties, and overall well-being, all medications have side effects. Some studies suggest that these treatments result in shorter adult height than what would have been attained without them; others list side effects like allergic reaction, blood clots, and exaggerated hormonal effects (like lots of extra hair growth, hair loss, swelling of the breast tissue, or bad acne, as if there's some sort of puberty poltergeist inhabiting the body). The other catch is that hormonal treatment might not make any difference at all, especially if started after age fourteen in boys, which is an absurd and ironic threshold given that the definition of delayed puberty *begins* at fourteen for boys. This last bit of data is very much in flux, though, with a bunch of new studies on the horizon assessing a variety of different hormone treatment variants. Still late-blooming boys remain, at least at the current moment, stuck in a treatment catch-22: on the one hand, beware of medications and use them only as a last resort; but then again, if you watch and wait, it may become too late for a medicine to have any effect.

Late blooming is hard for both boys and girls, but since girls tend to mature first, even the late ones usually don't finish last. It's almost always a boy who claims this crown. As more and more research looks at puberty in general, my fingers are crossed that the resources won't go only toward looking at why this stage is beginning earlier, because the latest 2.5% deserve answers of their own.

If you have a late-blooming son, do what you can to acknowledge the situation together. Three out of four of these guys will be declared robustly healthy after a slew of tests and scans. If that happens, while you may breathe a sigh of relief, your son may still see no light at the end of the developmental tunnel. Honor that. Understand it. Talk to him, point him to alternate resources like a counselor, coach, or even an older sibling, to protect his sense of self. Help him to harness the frustration or sense of disadvantage, because those skills will pay off in spades later on. And lean on your pediatrician or a pediatric endocrinologist to help you weigh the pluses and minuses of treatment. If he's fine with the situation, that's great for him; if he's not, that's completely understandable.

There will always be late bloomers—as I said at the start, one out of every forty is, by definition, at the tail end of these statistical curves. As a society, we have fully normalized early girl puberty, and we will likely do the same for boy development once people start recognizing it. If nothing else, this chapter is a call to normalize the other end of the spectrum, and to help alleviate concerns where they can be lifted.

How their bodies develop varies widely from kid to kid. Amazingly, though, brain maturity follows a far more predictable path. And it happens a whole lot slower than you might think.

HOW TO TALK TO BOYS ABOUT . . . LATE BLOOMING

1. ASK HIM HOW HE FEELS. If your son is a late bloomer, he may care about being late to the puberty party. Ditto if he's on the shorter end. Some parents fear that checking in about this stuff might actually create worry. But most boys tell me they are relieved to be asked something like: *I've noticed a bunch of your classmates are looking tall these days . . . Do you want to talk about it? Or: Geez, my car had quite a smell when I drove everyone home from practice the other day! Do you want me to promise to tell you when you start to smell?*

2. IF HE'S GOOD WITH IT, YOU SHOULD BE GOOD WITH IT! Some boys really don't mind being late bloomers. They feel relieved to be growing up slowly, or maybe they receive attention for being who they are. Either way, if late blooming doesn't bother your son, it shouldn't bother you—there's nothing wrong with it. That said, start talking to his pediatrician around age fourteen if development appears nonexistent, whether your kid cares or not.

3. DON'T OVERPROMISE. This one is very important because boys (and girls!) just want to know that they are going catch up with—or at least fit in with—their peers. While it usually ends up that way, sometimes the path to get there is very delayed. And there's no guarantee that any child is going to hit a certain mile-stone by a given age, let alone a specific height. So if he asks when his body is going to change, the most honest and powerful answer is *I don't know*. Then follow it up with a conversation starter like: *Do you want to talk about how it feels to be later than many of your friends? Because I am guessing you have feelings about it . . .*

Chapter Five
WHEN THEY LOOK LIKE ADULTS BUT DON'T THINK LIKE THEM

WHEN MY KIDS STARTED OUT IN grade school, I had this rule that they could only open the front door for five people: their three grandparents, their dad, and me. That's it. Only those five. (And all five had house keys, by the way.)

No, it didn't matter if the person ringing the bell was someone they had known since birth. In an effort to combat stranger danger, our rule was that the kids wouldn't open the door for *anyone* except those five people, otherwise leaving that job to the adult who was home with them. With this black-and-white mandate there was no chance, no matter the temptation, that my kids would swing the door open for some random person.

The rule wasn't just clear, it was drilled into them and reinforced regularly every few weeks. That's how you win at parenting, I used to tell parents in my office. Just set a limit and repeat it over and over again. Which is precisely what I did one afternoon, with just the three of us at home: I reviewed the directive for what seemed like the thousandth time, finishing with a dramatic deep look into their eyes and the capstone question "Got it?"

"Got it!" they replied in unison. At which point I walked down the hall to take a shower.

While I was in the bathroom, I thought I heard the doorbell ring. So I jumped out of the shower, threw on some clothes, and rushed to the front door. Here's what I found: standing *inside* my house was an Amazon deliveryman.

What?! I looked at my kids, poised in the entryway next to this complete stranger. They were smiling, but when they saw the look on my face their grins faded.

"What were you guys thinking?" I asked (okay, yelled). I was totally flustered. "Do you know what you did wrong?!"

My son, all of six at the time, looked at me and then his facial expression changed dramatically—I swear I could almost make out a lightbulb over his head.

"Oh, Mom," he said, "I am so sorry. You are always telling us to use our manners and we didn't introduce ourselves!" At which point he stuck out his hand and politely introduced himself to the random guy dressed in Amazon-wear. Clearly, wrong lightbulb.

There was a long pause.

"You really ought to tell your kids not to answer the door to strangers," the deliveryman said.

What was wrong with my kids?

That was several years ago. These days, my kids answer the door more freely, welcoming people they know beyond the core five, and well-versed in the knowledge that you don't open it to strangers. Plus, at the front entry to our house there now sits a gate with an intercom that rings through our phone line. Just the other day, my now-teenage daughter and I were standing in the kitchen. The gate bell rang and she lifted the phone receiver.

"Hello?" she said, giving me a look that only a teenage girl can give as she does something both mundane and necessary, yet still looking for credit. I couldn't hear the person on the other end, but after a matter of seconds watched as she buzzed him in.

"Who's here?" I asked, just as I caught a glimpse of the complete stranger walking up to our front door.

"I dunno." She shrugged. "I couldn't understand what he was saying, so I let him in."

I mean, seriously?!

If you have ever been wowed by your child's intelligence only to watch him do something so thoughtless, impulsive, dangerous, or frankly idiotic that you cannot believe you ever thought he might be brilliant, rest assured you are not alone. I am right there with you. Opening the door to strangers, repeatedly, is just the tip of the foolish-decision iceberg.

In fact, every parent I have ever met has wondered—often aloud—how their child could simultaneously be so smart and so dumb. The answer has to do with brain maturation. Development of the brain isn't directly connected to puberty, but it's important to consider them at the same time. That's because, as our kids start to look more adult, the world seems to expect them to *think* like grown-ups, even though their brains cannot reliably deliver adult-like decisions. Kids get better at decision-making over time, yes. But they literally aren't hardwired to weigh the long-term implications of their actions, particularly when faced with short-term pleasures. Which is why pretty much every parent with a child between the ages of birth and about thirty deals with some degree of bad decision-making at least some of the time. Maybe in your house it's much of the time.

How our kids think—or why they don't—is simply a function of their brain development, and that's what this chapter is all about. There are plenty of ways that being a boy plays into how the brain makes choices—the subject at the heart of the second half of this book—but for the next few pages, the goal is to master (or just get a grip on) the process of mental maturation independent of gender. If nothing else, understanding how the brain grows and changes gives us an enormous parenting leg-up through all of our kids' tween and teen years.

THE MATURATION OF THE TEEN BRAIN, VERY BRIEFLY

We uniformly accept that toddlers aren't consequential thinkers, but something happens when we drop our kids off on that first day of kindergarten and suddenly they seem grown up. Certainly by high school we credit them with consistently being able to make mature decisions. Well, they're not and they can't.

The reality is that these two processes of body and brain maturation run on completely separate clocks. Yes, there clearly exists some mutualism. For instance, the hormones of puberty cross into the brain and affect the way it manages information, sometimes quite profoundly. But the development of the brain—the way it organizes itself and maximizes its own efficiency—is almost entirely independent of the development of the body, with its shape-shifting and growing. Not to mention the brain takes a whole lot longer to develop than everything else south of it. In other words, even though our kids appear grown up, their mental maturity lags.

At the root of what is happening inside our kids' heads sit two brain basics: (1) growth and shrinkage, and (2) myelination. We'll dive deep into both, but a top-line overview helps set the stage:

> 1. **Growth and Shrinkage.** The brain grows and shrinks, grows again and shrinks again throughout childhood, and after that it pretty much just shrinks. This isn't necessarily a bad thing, though—in fact, it's quite key—because some of this shrinkage is highly specific and fundamental to honing skills that eventually make us expert at some things.

> 2. **Myelination.** Naked wires send signals very slowly compared with insulated ones. That's true in life, and it's true in the brain, too. This explains why the process of *myelination*—or slowly building a layer of in-

sulation around a nerve cell—can make the brain work more efficiently. And why kids whose brains are only partially myelinated, i.e., all kids, have parts of their brains (the fun! impulsive! sensation-seeking! parts) that work far better than others (the wise, cough, long-term, cough, weigh-the-consequences parts).

Now let's back up and get into some detail, starting with point #1: growth and shrinkage.

USE IT OR LOSE IT

Human babies are born with lots and lots of nerve cells inside their brains, on the order of 100 billion. Put into context, that means that a fetus grows 250,000 neurons every minute in the womb. Amazingly, new neurons continue to appear through the toddler years. Over time, *neuronal proliferation,* as it's technically called, winds down to a relatively slow trickle until the tween years, when there is a dramatic uptick in the thickening of many neurons. After age twelve, there are some small areas of the brain that are able to generate new cells and thicken, but by and large the total number of neurons begins a lifetime of dwindling. This notion that the brain grows in infancy and then accelerates its growth again around age eight or nine is relatively new—as recently as when I was in medical school, it was common knowledge that a person was born with all of the neurons they were ever going to have. Lots of common knowledge acquired in medical school gets disproven and thrown out over time, by the way.

Why does neuronal number matter? Because neurons are the physical workhorses of the brain, interconnecting with one another (a single neuron can connect with up to 10,000 others!) in order to produce thought, motion, emotion, and all the rest that happens up there. Babies and toddlers develop skills at shockingly fast rates. Then the frenzied pace of acquisition slows down slightly—to an amazingly rapid clip, let's say—until one day your third- or fourth-grader turns around and masters a board game or sport or building strategy or musical instrument at a speed and in a manner that takes you back to the leaps he made in his infancy. Is that a function of more neurons appearing in his head? Perhaps; but if so, only partially.

That's because as the brain is growing, and even when it's not, it actively whittles away any neurons that aren't being used. All of our brains have done this since birth and will continue doing so through the end of our lives. It's informally (and somewhat affectionately) called the "use it or lose it" phenomenon: if a neuron isn't utilized then it's wasting precious space inside a packed head, and it needs to go. The death of that cell isn't a bad thing at all, because it allows us to concentrate energy and resources on neurons that fire toward a particular goal. In other words, losing excess neurons helps us master the abilities facilitated by the ones remaining.

The brain also works hard to streamline the connections between neurons, deleting the links that aren't utilized. Because each neuron can connect with hundreds and even thousands of others, limiting these networks is critical to specialization. The fancy medical term for the loss of a connection between nerve cells is *synaptic pruning*—a synapse is the tiny space between two nerve endings, and "pruning" refers to that thing we do to trees to shape them, clearing away the overgrowth. (Now you can toss that phrase around and impress your friends, as in "My son's incredible *Fortnite* prowess seems to increase weekly . . . must be synaptic pruning!")

How does brain growth and shrinkage fit into the framework of parenting a child through puberty? Simply insofar as it helps to remember that becoming good at something, be it a language, physical skill, social interaction, or following a rule, takes time. Over many years, the brain physically shifts, cementing frequently trodden pathways and deleting those it doesn't use. So while your kid may grasp a lesson in a moment, it can take much longer for the knowledge to burn into his brain. And this explains why you might have to say something a thousand times before your kid really gets it.

BRAIN MESSAGING AT MAXIMAL SPEED

Now on to point #2: myelination. Myelin is made from fat cells that wrap around the outside of neurons. Naked neurons without myelin look gray, but myelinated ones look white thanks to the sheen of fat. The construction of a myelinated neuron is remarkably similar to your phone-charging cord, with the wire inside being the long arm of the nerve cell and the plastic coating around it the myelin. All of this matters because naked, unmyelinated neurons (just like naked, uninsulated wires) are quite slow at transmitting impulses; but once covered with an outer layer, a signal moves significantly faster—in the brain it's on the order of 3,000 times faster. The bottom line is this: a brain that can ping-pong information with maximal speed and efficiency is considered "mature," and since myelin speeds up signal transmission, it is a fair yardstick of maturity.

The brain myelinates itself very slowly and in a very specific sequence. This developmental pattern is gradual and linear, totally different from the development of the body through puberty. Below the neck, physical maturation happens relatively quickly—usually over about five or six years—and in no particular order. Hair, curves, voice changes, acne, body odor . . . they all seem to appear when they feel like it, starting sometime between seven and eleven years of age. Inside the brain, on the other hand, myelin lays itself down cell-by-cell like self-knitting leg warmers, beginning its trek before birth and taking decades to stretch out over billions of neurons.

For a long while now, scientists have known that myelin takes its sweet time to make its way through the brain. But just how slowly was historically underestimated. It used to be widely agreed upon that by the time a kid graduated from high school, his brain was fully mature. That was before researchers could look inside the brain with sophisticated imaging tools. Beginning in the 1990s, scientists used MRI scanners to create high-resolution pictures of the brain, building myelination maps and recharting the timeline for development. Because MRI is radiation-free, researchers could justify taking pictures of normal, healthy brains. The importance of this is hard to overstate: it's one thing when doctors and scientists use imaging techniques with significant risks (like radiation) to study sick bodies because there's a trade-off, a risk-benefit analysis in which the downside of a test is outweighed by the upside of figuring out what's going on; it's an entirely different thing when they are able to harness technology with very little risk in order to understand what's normal. Collecting information about illness is critical to the advancement of medicine, but so too is understanding typical development.

One researcher in particular, Jay Giedd, has followed a group of kids for twenty-five years, imaging more than 3,500 of them. He expected that when his subjects reached the end of their teen years his study of myelination would be complete. But the pictures told a very different story, which is why Giedd had to bring his subjects back year after year after year, all the way through college and their twenties. Their brains were still not done maturing, not until close to the age of thirty.

Giedd and his fellow researchers use computer-generated images of brains that can be tweaked into a rainbow of colors showing where myelin is most concentrated and where it's basically absent, a living map of brain maturation. Here's what they have documented over and over again: myelin moves upward and outward, from the bottom to the top and from the inside out. The first areas to mature are at the bottom of the brain nearest the neck and at the brain's central core, the regions controlling the most basic body functions like breathing, eating, and general movement. Myelin can be seen in these places starting as early as the third trimester of pregnancy, even before a baby is born. Through the infant and toddler years, myelin begins to march upward and outward, moving to the language and sensory centers, improving skills like vision, hearing, language development, and motor coordination. This was known long ago. Where Giedd's research in particular got really interesting was in the later years of adolescence.

By the tween years, myelin has fully occupied the middle-most part of the brain. Among other things, this is home to the emotional epicenter, an area called the limbic system. This region is filled with lots of different specific brain structures you may have heard about, like the amygdala, hippocampus, thalamus, and hypothalamus. In terms of function, the limbic system commands feelings, behaviors, motivations, and memories. It's the risk/reward region, the part that seeks novelty with its resultant emotional or physical high. By the time a kid hits middle school, his limbic system is pretty much fully mature, its neurons thoroughly insulated and therefore able to send and receive signals at warp speed. Kids this age can form memories they will keep for the rest of their lives; they are motivated by people around them and the stories they hear; they develop passions; they invent games and strategies; and they also happen to be really good at being impulsive and emotional. Thank you, limbic system.

You know what's *not* myelinated in middle school? The outermost part of the brain right underneath the forehead: the frontal lobe. Myelin just hasn't quite made it all the way out there yet. In fact, this is one of the very last parts of the brain that will mature, with the last of the last being the tip-top of the frontal lobe, the area called the prefrontal cortex.

The prefrontal cortex is where a person weighs the consequences of doing something versus not doing something—it is the part of the brain that helps make good, smart, big-picture decisions. Long-term decisions. The opposite of immediate-gratification decisions. It's where we process insight and empathy, control our impulses, and avoid risk-taking behaviors. The prefrontal cortex is the counterbalance to the limbic system—which is how it earned its nickname, "the brain's CEO." And what Giedd showed was that it's not going to be fully myelinated until at least a decade after the limbic system, and usually much later than that.

I am not saying that the prefrontal cortex in your child's brain is totally nonfunctional—not at all. The prefrontal cortex exists, packed with neurons completely capable of signaling one another. And we have all seen that in action in our kids: they are fully capable of thinking through scenarios, weighing consequences, and behaving cautiously. But the prefrontal cortex is not fully myelinated, while the neurons in the limbic system are. And that means that if two messages are sent simultaneously, one to the limbic system and one to the prefrontal cortex, then in the tween or teen brain the message going to the limbic system will arrive much faster—3,000 times faster. The prefrontal cortex just cannot be accessed as readily as the limbic system. And that means that our kids can and often will make emotional or impulsive decisions (like: *let's open the front door because someone is ringing the bell*) before weighing the consequences (like: *that guy at the front door is a total stranger and I have no idea what he wants*). The limbic system wins; thank you, myelin.

Plus, there is a bunch of data documenting that when kids are around their friends, the limbic system is even *more* engaged, as if it's on heightened alert. This is true of both friends in real life and virtual friends, which means that social media with its 24/7 clock has seemingly endless impact on the limbic system. Back in our day, peer pressure was relegated to the hours when we were physically with our friends or maybe talking to them on the phone, but today it exists nonstop. Turns out, giving a kid time to think through a decision in the presence of adults—or at least without other kids around—can allow him to access his prefrontal cortex in a way that being surrounded by a group of friends simply doesn't. This mental setup explains how a teenager can sit with his parents at the dinner table and promise not to drink at a party and really mean it, but then two hours later that very same kid, surrounded by his posse of pals, can wind up downing a beer or two or five.

In our adult brains, by contrast, completion of myelination means that a message can get to the prefrontal cortex as quickly as it can get to the limbic system, allowing those two areas to duke it out. Thinking about cheating? studying? speeding? putting on that helmet? saying yes? saying no? Once the entire brain is mature and signals arrive at all regions at essentially the same time, the brain's intended check-and-balance system can kick in, helping to drive "mature" decisions. Of course, lots of external influences can interfere, everything from alcohol, drugs, and medication to sleep deprivation to brain disease. But in a healthy, sober, mature adult brain, the prefrontal CEO can vie with the limbic system and will often win.

Giedd and others have shown that the prefrontal cortex doesn't fully mature until the mid- or late twenties—some say it may even be the early thirties—but meanwhile the emotional center is totally mature in the tween years, and it rules the young brain. Adults have balance between these two centers; tweens, teens, and twentysomethings simply don't.

The delayed maturation of the prefrontal cortex compared with the limbic system isn't all bad. Many evolutionary biologists and sociologists believe that having a brain ruled by the limbic system confers great benefits. Tweens and teens are willing and able to take risks that many adults cannot. I am not talking about foolish risks that create obvious danger, but rather the openness to try something new, to explore, to invent, to discover. Put this in the context of a brain that is growing and pruning, and it is easy to see how the young brain craves new information and can learn more, faster. Our kids are highly motivated, able to retain new knowledge, and wired to push boundaries because their brains are both flexible and absorbent. Just consider the modern-day example of the classic tech company founder—a twentysomething with a still-dominant limbic system—and you have a perfect example of how this combination has profoundly affected the human experience.

But until our kids use their insulation imbalance for good, or even while they do, we parents will worry about thrill-seeking and feel-good decision-making that can have major negative downstream consequences. Kids are hardwired to think— actually, not-think—this way. We should be a little worried, especially in today's world, and so should they. The whole point of understanding myelination in the context of brain maturation is to be able to reconcile why our smart kids can sometimes make dumb decisions. Once we do, we will realize there are parenting steps we can take to outsmart the hardwiring, minimizing the risk and maximizing the upside of this temporary anatomy.

KNOWLEDGE IS POWER

Yes, the brain develops along a well-choreographed course, independent of acne and breast budding and testicular growth. And yet the hormones that drive these adultifying physical changes do cross over into the brain, bathing the neurons— both unmyelinated and myelinated—in a novel stew. There exist very real hormonal effects on the brain, which in turn translate into emotional and physical shifts. This goes way beyond the stereotypical description of estrogen driving moodiness or testosterone prompting rage, both of which seem to be true, but not for all people and certainly not all of the time.

Hormones themselves have an intricate language through which they communicate, so that when the level of one is high, this triggers another hormone to either rise or fall, depending upon preexisting feedback loops. And as you know from Chapter 2, puberty begins in the brain, with the hypothalamus and pituitary glands releasing precursor hormones that trip the ON switch of a much bigger cascade. So while I have told you that puberty and brain development are entirely independent, the truth is that they simply run on separate, overlapping clocks— they do indeed impact each other.

And speaking of clocks, the fact that kids are entering puberty at increasingly young ages represents a layer that deserves to be added to this conversation. Earlier-onset puberty means that kids look more adult at increasingly young ages. Nine- and ten- and eleven-year-olds used to look like kids, but these days they resemble not exactly children but also not adults either . . . they are in between . . . they are tweens. Their body changes might occur earlier but brain development hasn't sped up; there exists no evidence of acceleration of synaptic pruning or myelination. In fact, if anything, scientists have recognized the opposite: brains mature more slowly than anyone ever thought, even in the context of bodies beginning to change more rapidly. And beyond the tween years, when kids are squarely in the teen zone, looking a whole lot like adults and allowed to do adult-like things (like drive or vote), they *still* have another decade before their brains are fully grown up.

Appreciating the contrast between the rapidity of physical changes and the snail's pace of brain maturation ultimately helps all of us, parents and kids, understand why tweens and teens sometimes make really good decisions but not always. And why people often look at our kids as if they *should* make great decisions because they look like grown-ups—or at least they are starting to—but they don't think like grown-ups.

Pausing is one of the most powerful tools in the face of incomplete myelination. If signals travel faster to the limbic system, messages just need a little more time to get to the rational prefrontal cortex. Seriously, just counting to ten before doing something impulsive can make all the difference in the world. Ultimately, understanding the *why* helps kids avoid foolish choices—it allows them a path to outsmart their own hardwiring. It also helps us parents to avoid putting our kids in scenarios for which they are simply not ready. And in the meantime, the benefits of the limbic system—from curiosity to innovation to passion—remain in place, readily accessible at the right moments.

I am a big advocate of teaching kids about brain maturation and myelin. If the knowledge helps us as parents, imagine the difference it makes to a kid who can understand the why of his behavior. If you feel like you cannot teach the topic yourself, just have your teenager read this chapter—kids constantly tell me that understanding the biology is the first step toward better decision-making.

It's also tremendously empowering for kids (and their parents) to appreciate the impact of pubertal hormones without feeling victimized by them. Hormones circulate throughout the body, and that means they impact the brain. Good to know. Better yet, we should all begin to identify how these chemicals make us feel—in puberty and beyond. That way, we can anticipate and manage those feelings.

Ideally, we will avoid putting our sons' brains in situations they cannot handle. This is where the word "no" comes in handy. If your son is asking to hang out with a friend who has been getting into trouble lately, or if he's begging to go to a party where there will be no supervision, or even if he just wants to keep his phone in his room each night and you know he cannot resist the temptation to be on it endlessly . . . say no. He will give you all the right reasons for why you shouldn't worry, but that's his prefrontal cortex talking. Outside of your home, or even just behind a closed bedroom door, peer influence turns up the volume of his limbic system. Why put our kids in situations where their brains will be primed to choose a worrisome path? There will be plenty of scenarios where our sons will find themselves in over their heads, so let's help them to opt out of the ones that can be anticipated. The prefrontal cortex won't mature any faster if it's put into tricky situations.

Bad choices can result from the developmental fact that tween and teen brains just can't make the smartest decisions in the moments when their limbic systems dominate. This is why their choices can be so different depending upon where they are or who is asking a particular question. It all comes down to pruning and myelination, which they are in the middle of.

HOW TO TALK TO BOYS ABOUT . . . BRAIN DEVELOPMENT

1. CONNECT BIOLOGY WITH DECISION-MAKING. It really helps kids to understand that our parenting choices are related to their ability to make smart decisions. It's not that we don't trust them (though sometimes we don't trust them) but rather that we don't trust their brains to do the right thing. And with good reason! So explain brain maturation as best you can, read this chapter together, or find a video online that explains the topic clearly (for older kids who like videos, I always recommend *SciShow* by Hank Green).

2. TEACH PAUSING STRATEGIES SO THAT MESSAGES CAN GET TO THE PREFRONTAL CORTEX, TOO. Teach your son (or daughter!) to take a moment before making a choice that's not obviously smart and safe. How? Count to ten, or breathe in and out slowly for a few breaths, or, if time allows, take a longer break to go for a walk, shoot some hoops, journal . . . whatever helps to clear the mind. This is a real thing by the way, and allows for more even distribution of signaling throughout the brain.

3. START WITH THE POSITIVE. There's a reason the most successful bosses, teachers, and other voices of authority begin a tough conversation with a note of praise: it makes criticism easier to receive. So if your son has been making poor decisions, don't start a conversation by diving right into the dark deep end of the pool. Try to give a little bit of love first. Tell him how proud you are that he rocked his math test before you lay into him about spending three hours gaming, not to mention the scraps of food and dirty socks left behind at the scene. Or thank him for doing the dishes before you remind him to clean up his room. This approach can be a game changer. It can also be tough advice to follow if he's done something really egregious—in those cases it's fine to not start with praise!

Part Two
OUTSIDE FORCES

Chapter Six
BOYS AND "THE TALK": 21ST-CENTURY INFORMATION DISRUPTORS

PUBERTY'S SEEMINGLY ENDLESS ROAD IS ABOUT becoming curvy, hairy, stinky, and moody. But hanging out in the not-so-distant future—maybe your son is even there already—sits its endpoint: the ability to make a baby. Even though a long stretch of puberty has very little to do with sex at all, still, at some point every kid will experience new sexual urges powered by the very same hormones that make him physically transform. So basically, while puberty starts off as the slow, highly individualized story of the metamorphosis of one person's body, by its very nature it will eventually prime that person to want to interact with other bodies. And that means, if we are going to explore the entire gamut of this stage of life, we cannot *not* talk about sex.

But sex is an endpoint, and our kids need to accumulate a mass of information along the way to it, everything from basics about self-care to myth-busters about body products that overpromise. There is so much to cover, in fact, that parents have developed radically different ideas about the agenda. Many assume their kids will receive chunks of body education in school, or at the very least will absorb it from the world around them. Still most will tackle some of this information themselves.

From my earliest days as a pediatrician, I have always asked teenagers whether they talk to their parents about anything puberty- or sex-related, mostly because the information gap amazes me. Over and over, from boys and girls alike, I hear a version of: *Nope. We have never talked about any of this stuff.* They acquire their knowledge from music or media or real-life friends, all the more compelling because it is uttered by not their mother or their father. Very occasionally, the opposite is true—emphasis on "very," especially when it comes to sex.

Then, when I sit down with parents in the absence of their kids, I ask the same question. Nearly 100% of them reply, aghast, *Of course!* Even though I don't ask for clarification, many will launch into a (sometimes excruciatingly) detailed account of their deft delivery of The Talk, that infamous powwow about sex. This experience repeats itself so regularly, it didn't take me long to learn that there is a major disconnect between most parents and children when it comes to talking about puberty. And regarding sex in particular—perhaps the most pivotal conversation for an adult, a major parenting milestone and hurdle cleared—the moment often doesn't even register with their kid.

Oof.

This dichotomy has landed us in an awkward place. As a society, we certainly have grown comfy talking in intimate detail about the lives of celebrities, political figures, and complete strangers alike. But in navigating the minefields of our own kids' bodies and intimacy, the equation shifts dramatically. Chatting about people outside of our homes—especially their sex lives—feels like fair game (and a fun game at that!), but under our own roofs many want to either dive as far into the sand as possible or just hold their noses and get the conversation over with.

Unfortunately, this double standard leaves our kids, for lack of a better word, screwed.

The goal of this chapter is to shine a light on what kids need to know about the path to sex, how they get those "facts," and the different ways the information is parsed out to guys and girls. Because the world is a very different place fom the one we grew up in, and these days information is not hard to come by. While this may not surprise you (it shouldn't, actually, because . . . Internet), what may rock your world is this: your primary competition for the sex education of your child is not another kid at school, or a teacher assigned to cover the birds and the bees, or even a "mature" book or magazine. No, it's online content because . . . Internet. When you first became a parent, stressors appeared in the form of managing dirty diapers and navigating tantrums. Now, you only wish.

We can't keep our kids safe and healthy if we don't open our eyes to how the content environment has shifted over the past couple of decades—both body and sex ed provide primo examples here. That said, it's not all doom and gloom! Yes, there's a hefty dose of imagery that you will work hard to deflect (aka porn, a topic big enough to warrant its own chapter). But there also exists a whole new world of educational content, much of it dressed up in the form of entertainment, readily available when you need an alternative voice to chime in. This teaching no longer falls squarely on you or the middle school science teacher, even if you wish it did. So let's head down the path to sex, when and how to talk about it, and whom else to invite into the conversation.

WHAT KIDS NEED TO KNOW, AND WHO SHOULD TEACH THEM

Some parents welcome talking about body changes and sex with open arms, but many others can't even imagine being ready to take these issues on, particularly with boys. This gender divide is reinforced by human nature's tendency to address what we see over what we know (or at least suspect). Since early female puberty is so visible, with young girls developing breasts or becoming curvy or falling into some super-stereotypical drama, most parents easily recognize it: *Aha! Hormonal influence! Must be puberty. Maybe we should talk about that. And oh my gosh, people are looking at my daughter like a sexual object. Gulp, looks like we need to talk about that, too . . .*

Meanwhile, puberty in boys of the same age is, for all intents and purposes, invisible. As Chapter 3 explained, that's why we often don't know they're in it. They just look taller (if even that—sometimes they simply look L-shaped, with their puppy-esque feet and still-squat legs) and have a slight stench about them (we still want to cuddle, though, so we generally get over it). Our boys' lack of overt pubescence allows us to pretend we don't need to address any of this just yet . . . It's probably too much for their immature brains . . . We'll get there when they are ready, and they neither look nor act ready. Cue the fart antics.

The initial subtlety of boy puberty often delays the start of conversations with our sons, and by the time many parents realize it, we are late to the game. Some of us don't even have the chance to cover the basics about what's happening, and why our boys are transforming, before it's suddenly time for the big conversations about what they will do with these new bodies. Sex is the culmination of puberty, the ultimate brass ring, and the reason why the descriptor "sex ed" has such staying power. But this doesn't describe the entirety of what our kids should learn, not by a long shot. So what do they need to know? When? And who should teach it?

They need to understand all of it, eventually, from the physical changes of puberty to the emotional and reproductive consequences. It's these repercussions that have compelled most schools to take on the responsibility of tackling body and sex ed. And that's because the people who *should* be teaching it— parents, guardians, and primary caretakers—often don't. Historically, they have feared giving bad information or dreaded the awkwardness; some were raised to believe that talking about these topics is shameful. So the content got outsourced to schools where, depending upon the state a child lives in and the type of school he attends, classes might cover any number of topics along the span from the debut of hormones all the way to intercourse. But there's nothing uniform about the way any of this stuff is taught.

For instance, schools use wildly different definitions of "sex." Some talk about sex as in gender, or the categories into which members of any given species are divided depending upon re- productive function. Others—most, actually—also address sex as the physical intimacy between two (or more) people that takes a wide variety of forms, and may or may not include inter- course with the goal (or side effect, depending upon perspec- tive) of reproduction. While a kiss is not sex, an unwanted kiss is sexual harassment, so these days teachers tend to keep the conversation broad. Often not *too* broad, though—some courses do not cover sex as in sexuality or sexual orientation; nor do they cover sexual language and imagery, as in phone sex or sex texts (aka *sexting*), even though these can be highly arousing. Basically, when describing what's taught in a typical sex ed class in school, much of the time we're talking about sex the activity, not the identity, and in the flesh rather than photos or videos. The semantics are important, because when it comes to dia- logues with our kids about sex, the last thing any of us want to do is dive into a big conversation in which we think we are talk- ing about *doing it* while they think we are talking about identify- ing as a male or a female. Miscommunication happens. More often than you think.

Just as the *sex* in "sex ed" can mean many different things, there's nothing uniform about the *ed* part either. The rules about what can (or cannot) be taught in schools vary by state, with year-by-year sex education requirements outlined precisely the same way guidelines are set for less controversial subjects like history and math. This means that the content taught in California can be quite different from what is taught in Mississippi, despite the fact that the hormonal transformation of the students in these classrooms is the same.* So, how much is discussed and precisely when depend entirely on where you live. It's also worth noting that some state standards apply only to public schools, meaning all bets are off when it comes to what is taught on certain topics in private and parochial classrooms.

Body and sex ed can, in theory, incorporate countless potential lessons. The awesomeness of this task may explain why many schools limit themselves to the classic definition of sex (the action, not the label), and by extension equate sex education with exclusively heterosexual intercourse education. A broader interpretation of sex feels too sprawling for many schools—and even many parents—to manage. But this restrictive definition, while more surmountable, is too limited to accomplish what kids need; in order to be adequately educated, they must learn about a whole lot more than intercourse. All of this leaves schools in an impossible position when it comes to teaching about sex or, frankly, about any of the risky tween and teen behaviors we all aim to minimize.

Educators, by and large, know that kids are starving for information, especially given the earlier beginning of body development, and the current climate of access to more info at increasingly young ages. They also understand that the first to inform often makes the biggest impact, regardless of whether that information comes from a trained educator or a random video packed with incorrect or outlandishly graphic content.

---

* While many schools have begun to incorporate "wellness" curricula starting as young as kindergarten or first grade, these courses focus mostly on topics like hand washing, nutrition, and sleep. Body teaching as in genitalia and physical development tends not to appear until around fifth grade, by which time, it is worth noting, the vast majority of kids in the class have already entered puberty and some girls have even started their periods. The covered content rapidly amps up from there and can include everything from bullying to violence to drugs to, yes, sex. Though, here again, the content is often heterosexual sex.

And layered on top of this, teachers on the frontlines of school-based sex ed know that the class they teach may be, for some kids, the very first formal conversation about *anything* puberty- or body-related, especially among boys. It can be a big leap from silently wondering how big your penis is going to be to learning how to use it responsibly. Dedicated educators understand all this and want to do right by their students.

For many years, debates have raged over whether sex ed should be taught in the school or left to be managed at home, with some parents wanting control over the entire conversation (understandably) and others who feel the exact opposite (*I don't want to teach that! You do it!*), while a third group, perhaps the largest, really doesn't give much thought to the issue at all (until they get that letter from school announcing the upcoming class, in which case most develop strong instantaneous opinions). If you've never thought about what schoolteachers contend with as they tackle the oft-dreaded sex ed curriculum, maybe now you'll feel a bit more sympathy.

DO PARENTS DO A BETTER JOB OF TEACHING THIS STUFF THAN SCHOOLS?

We parents haven't necessarily succeeded where schools have stumbled. Most parents tell me that their goal for both their sons and their daughters is for them to have healthy, loving, passionate, and positive relationships—with themselves and with others—throughout their lives. But just as teachers struggle with the content, tone, and approach of body teaching in general and sex in particular, so too do parents—sometimes more so.

A one-on-one setting can place tremendous pressure on a talk about what's happening to the body; and when it comes to covering sex, the stakes can feel much higher. Often this leads to the parental instinct to make sex as unappealing as possible, with some parents talking about sex stoically and formally and others approaching it like it's the plague. But the not-so-subliminal message that *this conversation is no fun, and neither is sex!* fails to delay most kids' sexual experimentation. In fact, it stands a serious chance of backfiring, because we all know that sex isn't a bad thing, and it isn't an emotionless affliction either. Demonizing it doesn't guarantee that they'll delay the act; all it does is heap on a layer of shame, with the added bonus of significantly reducing the likelihood that our kids will talk to us about their intimate relationships down the road. Somehow, though, it's painfully difficult to avoid negativity, especially when your audience of one—your offspring, who himself is a consequence of sex—offers you a limited attention span.

We parents all lived our own version of puberty, but most of us can hardly remember the bulk of it. This skews, and at times deeply flaws, our approach with our kids. Yeah, yeah, yeah, we can all recall some peak or trough moments like they were yesterday. But we often rely upon these as if they represent the totality of the process. Meanwhile, many of our experiences have been packed away in the deep recesses of our subconscious.

Typically, among the most vivid and accessible memories of puberty are snippets of our sex education. Whether it was an intense conversation with our own parent or a mocked class at school, or a vital piece of intel gleaned from a pal or from that pal's *Playboy* magazine, when prompted most of us can conjure up at least one memory of how we were informed on the topic. For me: sex ed Poster Day, when small groups presented all you needed to know about a given form of birth control—the foam poster was a mess. We recall mostly images, because that's the way the brain works, and ultimately these memory films transform into cautionary tales or relatable life lessons for our kids. The path to homegrown, parent-taught sex ed is far from objective, data driven, even predictable. There aren't standards or curricula for parents to follow, and as a result we each teach this content our own way. This would be a winning solution if only all parents actually engaged in the conversations, and really taught the content. While our generation does a far better job of approaching it than our own parents ever did, still, for a zillion different reasons—ranging from our own hang-ups to the fear of getting it wrong—much of this teaching doesn't happen at home.

THE REINVENTION OF BODY AND SEX ED

Taken together, decades of controversies around teaching body and sex ed in schools and at home has created a market for something new. Plus, the way sex ed in particular was taught to many of us—a dry and dreaded one-off—certainly stood for a reboot. And so, without any one person in charge, this life curriculum has received a sort of makeover: The Talk (singular) has been replaced with multiple conversations over many years, recognizing a continuum of body education and sex information. Parents and teachers suddenly are no longer the only ones considered qualified to pass along this knowledge; and somewhere along the line, it became A-OK to acknowledge that even though the subject of sex is serious, it's also awkward and funny and occasionally absurd.

Newfangled body and sex ed encourages our kids to be part of a two-way conversation, allowing adults to be educated in return on topics ranging from terms we have never heard before to what dating life is really like for our kids' generation. And these interactive, none too serious meet-them-where-they-are techniques have been mastered by a new slate of educators: YouTubers, comedians, and animated characters alike, a small army of entertainers-meets-educators who have created loud, and it turns out extremely effective, voices in this field. They are disruptors, atypical messengers (many are nonparents and completely untrained in education, let alone biology or sex education) whose messages play out on computers and mobile devices across the country. They have largely replaced eager-beaver parents offering up explanations about what's going on down there, or the poor PE coach tapped to teach the birds and the bees in school. And it's all happened over the last several years.

We can trace this educational reinvention to more than a decade ago, when then–college student Laci Green posted a video reviewing a specific form of birth control. It turned out that a surprising number of people wanted to hear what she had to say. Green's YouTube channel, founded in 2008, built a steady following as she broadened the scope of her content to include sex-positive educational videos. By 2012, she was a spokesperson for Planned Parenthood, lecturing across the United States. By 2014, at the ripe age of twenty-five, she had over a million subscribers to her YouTube channel; had created a series with MTV; and her monthly video reach exceeded five million people in over a hundred countries. Today, it is estimated that Green's videos have been viewed well over 150 million times. Basically, she invented the field of online sex ed—or, at the very least, she scaled it for a mass audience.

Green paved the road for an almost unanticipated movement: largely female YouTubers and vloggers (that's video bloggers, for those not in the know) offering sex ed for the young masses.* Today, there's a large flock of content creators like Laci, most of them producing some version of what she started, which is to say short-form videos tackling one topic at a time, from the most basic concepts that might be taught in a fifth-grade classroom to highly specific anatomical or acrobatic sex

---

* A parallel movement was emerging among teen YouTubers, though it wasn't exactly sex ed. This group, led by early pioneers like Bo Burnham, posted videos covering topics from body changes to relationships. But these early vloggers aimed purely to entertain other kids, not formally educate them. Viewing them now, these posts feel almost like recorded journal entries—memoirs of life in middle and high school. They tell stories that resonated with millions of viewers and continue to do so, all these years later.

tips. These videos—and their narrators-cum-protagonists—all share an educational bent, delivering answers to widely sought questions. They also share a similar format (talking head with interspliced animations or show and tell–style models), pace (almost always a rapid clip), and vibe (the cool-meets-bubbly young hosts—usually female—seem to have endless energy on all topics).

The popularity of Green's videos and the entire genre she inspired proved there was a hole in the market: people wanted information about their bodies and sex. Not just teenagers, by the way—lots of adults are online watching these videos as well. But even though they have generated countless hours of up-beat, some would even say aspirational, content, these videos still fall squarely in the realm of education. Are they effective? Yes. Popular? Yes. But entertaining to the point of virality? Not the goal. And designed for younger kids? With few exceptions, no. This explains why the people who consume this sex ed content are often older teens and adults seeking out specific information—they actively want to be educated, but not in the middle school sense of the word.

Then came a second and arguably larger group of viewers combing the Web not for education, but rather for enlighten-ment or just some general—and generally intriguing—information sometimes related to sex, oftentimes not. These folks congregate on sites like TED (short for Technology, Enter-tainment, and Design), a thirty-five-year-old organization founded with the goal of sharing "ideas worth spreading." TED is far older than YouTube or even Laci Green for that matter, originating as an invitation-only in-person speakers' series. But the conference's impact multiplied severalfold when, in 2006, it moved to include an online format. Today easily downloadable TED Talks cover almost every conceivable topic—yes, includ-ing sex.

Way back in 2010, just as Laci Green's channel was picking up some serious steam, the comedian Julia Sweeney appeared in a TED Talk. Sweeney, a *Saturday Night Live* alum, offered up a hilarious account of the time she found herself inadvertently giving her eight-year-old daughter The Talk. It all began innocently enough when Sweeney and her daughter got into a conversation about reproduction among frogs, which had been covered earlier that day at school. One thing led to another over the course of the evening, somehow culminating with Sweeney and her daughter watching a video of mating cats and then dogs and the inevitable question: *Mom, do you think they would have on the Internet any humans mating?* Sweeney's humble yet laugh-out-loud-funny retelling of how she accidentally led her own child to ask about online porn is worth a watch if you aren't one of the 3.5 million people who have already seen it.

Sweeney wasn't the only—or even the first—comic to appear online poking fun at sex. But she was one of the first to break through using an education-ish platform, in this case TED, and she succeeded because her "idea worth spreading" boiled down to a version of every parent's greatest fear: being fundamentally unnerved when the inevitable Talk snuck up completely unexpected. Her humanity feels familiar; her humiliation too. We have all found ourselves spiraling deeper and deeper into some conversation or other with our child that we couldn't get back on the right track; Sweeney just retold hers better than any of us could. And, in the relatively early days of shared online content, she modeled the attitude that laughing about sex in general and The Talk in particular isn't just a relief, it's an effective teaching tool.

Sweeney's tale of parenting-gone-sideways-when-it-comes-to-sex-ed was more relatable than intentional, making her an accidental teacher. And this, it turns out, is key to reaching audiences that are looking for inspiration over education. Unlike Laci Green and her cadre of polished, semi-scripted sex teachers, Sweeney didn't necessarily mean to become one. She simply told a universal story, resonating with genuineness. And so, over the years, people have found their way to Sweeney's

TED Talk (and many similar variations on the theme, some even funnier) not just because they wanted to learn about how to talk about sex—or, rather, how *not* to—but also because they wanted to be amused. When entertainment drives viewership and the premise just happens to be sex, unanticipated audiences often show up. When they do, they tend to learn something. It's accidental sex ed, and it's surprisingly effective.

Which is precisely what happened in 2017 with the launch of *Big Mouth*. This animated show about puberty aired on Netflix and became instantly popular among the middle and high school set, even though it wasn't created for them (certainly not the younger among them) or meant to be a source of valid information (this was not edutainment by design). *Big Mouth* not only provided accidental sex ed, it did so for an unintentionally young audience who needed—and wanted!—the info.

Don't get me wrong: *Big Mouth* is nothing like Julia Sweeney's TED Talk or like any of Laci Green's videos, for that matter. Rather, it's a cartoon show, with episodes running around half an hour each, set during puberty much the same way that a World War Two series might be set in 1940s Europe. The series chronicles best friends Nick and Andrew—who may be the same age, go to the same school, and share the same group of friends, but currently live in vastly different bodies. While Andrew is leagues ahead of Nick in puberty, both boys desperately struggle to manage what their hormones are (or aren't) delivering. Written through the lens of adults looking back at the horrors of this stage in their lives, and intended for audiences who want to cringe-laugh at their own adolescence, *Big Mouth* retells painful, profanity-ridden stories of puberty, magnifying every physical and emotional—not to mention sexual—insult.

The last thing its creators Nick Kroll and Andrew Goldberg (yes, they *are* Nick and Andrew) imagined was that *Big Mouth* would become a significant source of middle school educational content. If you doubt that, you need only to watch the Season 1 trailer, which, in two short minutes, covers everything from masturbation to oral sex to a talking vagina, with plenty of swearing thrown in for extra measure. No surprise the show earned a TV-MA rating—and that was fine by Nick and Andrew in real life.

The team behind *Big Mouth* never intended to be sex educators. They were a group of talented Hollywood writers and actors using the premise of puberty and the platform of animation as the basis for a purely entertaining show. As Andrew (the human, not the cartoon) described the early trajectory: "We started off writing the show for ourselves and what was funny. And then I remember, before it came out—but after the trailer came out—there were these comments like: 'This is a show for kids that kids can't watch. Who is it for?' And for the first time, I was like, 'Oh no! We made a show for nobody?!' But that now seems not to be the case."

Indeed, the case is this: they made a show for nobody that appealed to just about everybody. Well, at least everybody puberty-adjacent.

Within months of its debut, *Big Mouth* became an entertainment superstorm for tweens and teens everywhere. Combining the individual forces at play for both Green and Sweeney—informational content (that would be Green and her set) enmeshed with highly relatable humor (Sweeney and all the other comics stomping this ground)—*Big Mouth* added a new key ingredient in the annals of this particular genre of education: irreverence aimed squarely at adolescence and, incidentally, adolescents. Its mash-up of real-life biological trajectory and raw self-ridicule (and have I mentioned the foul language?) streamed seamlessly across the Netflix platform onto phones and laptops coast to coast.

No one knows quite how popular *Big Mouth* really is, thanks to Netflix's famously zip-lipped policy about data and viewership. That said, it ranked in the Top 20 most-watched Netflix shows in 2018. Ask any teenager you know, and you will quickly gain a sense of the show's reach. Not only do virtually all teens know what *Big Mouth* is, each one I have asked feels deep kinship with a favorite character experiencing some familiar adolescent insult. The anticipated dreaded scenarios of puberty, from bloodstained white shorts to the revelation of just how big your best friend's penis has become, play out with such irreverence it's hard to avert one's eyes, whether the viewer is done with puberty or just at the start.

It helps that along with co-creators Jennifer Flackett and Mark Levin, the inventors of *Big Mouth* currently parent four children among them, spanning the ages of pre-puberty to deep-in-the-thick-of-it. This means that Kroll, Goldberg, Flackett, and Levin are writing stories looking back on their own coming of age while simultaneously sitting in front-row seats watching the next-generation twenty-first-century version play out.

PUTTING THE "HE" IN HEALTH EDUCATION

Beyond its no-holds-barred approach, masturbation-focused story lines, and profanity-riddled dialogue, what really makes *Big Mouth* stand out from everything that has preceded it in the arena of general health, body, and sex ed is the show's gender POV. *Big Mouth* skews decidedly male.

For whatever reason, the vast majority of informational online content, from physical transformations to orgasm, tends to lean female.* Maybe it's thanks to menstruation, whose hot topic status in middle school comes from the fact that half of all girls must manage periods before they even become teenagers. Menstruation teaching goes hand-in-hand with sex ed curricula in grade school for good reason. Over time, the content levels out, so by high school conversations about STDs, consent, and even pregnancy feel relatively gender-neutral. But in the begin-

---

* It's worth noting here that I don't consider pornography informational online content. Curious about that statement? There's a whole lot more in the next chapter.

ning, a health class can seem heavily weighted toward girl issues and plumbing.

With the ascent of online educators like Laci Green, woven
into the content these days is a clear thread of female empowerment. Nothing wrong with that in the least—in fact, in many
ways "hooray!" for both the female owners of this biological
equipment and the males wanting to understand more about it.
But the skew adds to the hunt to find male-focused body info. It's
nearly impossible to search up legitimate male-oriented sex ed.

Big Mouth represents a major departure. The show revolves
around two boys, Nick and Andrew, and their larger group of
mostly guy friends. Even their testosterone-fueled urges get
characters: the Hormone Monsters, personifications of their
inner maleness and feelings of desire. As Nick (Kroll, not cartoon Nick) said almost wistfully one day when we spoke by
phone, "Hopefully a Hormone Monster becomes a tool or a
platform for boys to talk about stuff."

It's not that *Big Mouth* doesn't tackle female issues; it certainly does . . . and the Hormone Monstress is a serious force
to contend with. But the show *really* dives into the deep end for
males, so much so that the majority of the physical, emotional,
and hormonal struggles on *Big Mouth* flow from testosterone.
Almost every episode leads viewers down a path of thinking a
lot about what it's like to grow up as a guy.

"We have rightly spent so much energy making up for lost
time empowering girls over the last ten or twenty years that,
though the resources shouldn't be finite, we have kind of for-
gotten about boys a little," Goldberg told me, explaining the
show's XY bent. "And I think that boys feel it, especially with
the rise of the #MeToo movement. Even in progressive spaces
now, boys feel a little uncomfortable speaking up, because they
feel like they are supposed to have entitlement shame as well."

In many ways, the formalization of body and sex ed into
school curricula helped girls trade embarrassment and even
shame for knowledge and power. A typical school health class

talks a lot about female physiology, and girls at that age tend to be particularly good about talking right back. *Big Mouth* offers boys a path to the same end. The show looks on its surface to be unabashed and, well, big mouthed, but at its core it's about silence. As Kroll describes it, "I think that the more that boys— and girls—stay quiet and aren't able to talk about what they are going through, the more they build the foundation for shame which leads to some much sideways activity down the line."

Kroll and his co-creators have lifted the veil on the fact that boys enter puberty and have questions, lots of questions. They also have pride and bravado and discomfort and awkwardness. They are quieter than they used to be, at least many of them are, despite the fact that their inner Hormone Monsters yell loudly. *Big Mouth* tells boys that it's normal to wonder all of these things and feel all of these feelings. More than that, the show illustrates for girls that boys in fact have similarly deep inner worlds, filled with many of the same curiosities and con- cerns. It encourages kids to talk about their worries and mis- conceptions (and victories, too), regardless of gender. It reminds adults—and yes, lots of adults watch *Big Mouth*—of their stuffed-down, revised personal histories, encouraging them to refocus their parenting lens when it comes to how their kids might actually feel during this stage of life. Along the road through puberty, *Big Mouth* may be one of the best teachers our kids have because it speaks the truth, albeit in an exaggerated manner, dressed up in the cloak of a cartoon, foul-mouthed, sexually explicit, and slightly obsessed with masturbation.*

---

* During the year I spent writing this book, shows based on puberty became almost the norm, at least on streaming services. Along with *Big Mouth*, *Sex Education* and *PEN15* topped the list of most popular. While each of these shows takes on the subject completely differently—live action versus anima- tion; drama versus comedy—they have, as a group, made an even bigger im- pact than *Big Mouth* ever could have as a stand-alone. Best of all, they each start conversations in different ways, appealing to kids across a variety of back- grounds. The future of body and sex education continues to evolve before our very eyes.

EVEN THOUGH THERE ARE GREAT RESOURCES OUT THERE, PARENTS STILL PLAY A BIG ROLE HERE . . .

If you have learned anything from this chapter, it's that body and sex education are everywhere these days. Our role as parents is to jump into the conversations, plural. But when, how often, and what precisely to say?

Like most pediatricians, I firmly believe in parsing out information when your child is developmentally capable of receiving it. But today's kids live in a world overflowing with sexual imagery and language. They deserve to understand how to manage the onslaught, which often arrives before readiness. Not to mention, if the oft-quoted statistic is true and half of all eleven-year-old boys have seen online porn, then there is a mandate to accelerate.

Kids are entitled to facts—they need them in order to remain safe and healthy. But generally speaking, they can only absorb this information (at least as it is intended to be understood) when it is parsed out in an age-appropriate way. This is why many introductory "Welcome to Puberty!" books meant for kids at the starting line of the process completely avoid the topic of sex—I know; I have written a bunch of them. Puberty is, after all, the body's long path through reproductive development, along which kids morph into adults. The journey takes five, six, seven years . . . and mental maturity much longer. Front-loading sex ed doesn't necessarily work.

There isn't a magical age when we should start talking about sex with our kids. Parents often ask me for one, mostly because the structure of a right time makes the enormity of the conversation a little less daunting. I wish I could hand you a timeline checklist, but there is no such thing. I will say, though, that there is always at least one kid in your son's orbit—That Kid—who is filled with lots of salacious information, and there's no way of knowing whether your child is going to be on the receiving end of That Kid's "truth" about the Tooth Fairy or Santa

Claus or the birds and the bees. In general, my advice is to try to preempt That Kid.

Most schools begin health education classes around fourth or fifth grade, so it helps to cover some of the content before friends in the class feel inspired to take the opportunity to share their bonus information. As for younger kids who have older siblings or older influences in their lives (think: cousins, bus mates, or neighborhood friends), you may want to start by telling your own child that he will hear information about his body from other kids, and he can always come to you for the genuine truth. This spares you jump-starting conversations about intimacy when it really is too early for your kid to process them.

For the nervous Nellies in the crowd, there exist some basic mechanics of (talking about) sex—I have listed my own favorites below. Above all, give yourself a break if a talk doesn't go seamlessly, because we all screw it up at some point along the way: we all say things we don't mean to say, or we judge our kids' questions (sometimes silently, but we're still judging and they completely know it), or we open ourselves up for a question we really don't want to answer. Ultimately, every family approaches this subject in the way that is most comfortable—or least uncomfortable—for them. Leave your judgment behind and focus on your own child's enlightenment.

When we were kids, if our parents didn't talk about what was happening to our bodies (many didn't) and our schools didn't teach about it (again, most didn't), then we were left to seek out information from either our friends or a textbook with a few clinical diagrams, and both the friends and the books seemed to evoke in equal parts disgust, fear, and confusion. Silence around these topics was not at all a good thing—"horrible" might be a better word for it, considering the general lack of access to facts. That said, back in the day when information was more limited, the silver lining was a lack of TMI.

Fast-forward to parenthood in the twenty-first century. Our kids are managing all the same physiological and emotional by-products of hormones that we contended with decades ago. But today they are simultaneously bombarded by images and messages that sexualize them to a degree we never experienced—nor could we ever have imagined—when we were their age.

The new leaders of the body- and sex-ed movement aren't looking to replace your voice in your child's head, though sometimes they may; rather, they just want to acknowledge what's happening under the hood. In doing so, they are able to meet our kids where they're (hormonally) at, jump-starting their education often well before we might recognize their thirst for it. It may surprise parents to hear a pediatrician praising uncredentialed online teachers or series that dive deep into the waters of inappropriateness. But, for boys in particular, this subgenre is more than informational—it releases conversations around puberty and sex into the zeitgeist, making it watershed.

HOW TO TALK TO BOYS ABOUT . . . SEX

1. TIMING. On the one hand, information is power, so do it early. On the other, you wouldn't ice a cake before it was fully baked, so don't give him too much too soon. You get to choose when to start talking with your kid, but remember that these days he has lots of alternate sources, so delaying your conversation doesn't necessarily delay the flow of information.

2. MAKE THE TALK PLURAL. Talking about sex with your kid is no longer one-and-done, no matter how much you might wish. Cover one topic at a time, and repeat each topic many times over several years. Trust me when I tell you, the more often you go there, the

easier it becomes. We know this subject—we've *had* sex—we can handle most of what comes our way.

3. STICK WITH BROAD DEFINITIONS. That starts with defining terms! Sex is intimate physical contact involving the genitals. Don't forget to cover sex with one's self (aka masturbation) and all of the fooling around that precedes sex—those "bases" from our youth are intimate, too, and deserve some dialogue.

4. DON'T CHECK YOUR EMOTIONS AT THE DOOR. It's as important to dive into the emotional component of dating (or, frankly, not dating) as it is to cover the mechanics of physical intimacy. Our kids are growing up in a hookup culture where, at least in many cases, intimacy has no strings attached—in theory, that is. In reality, emotions travel alongside physical pleasure, so help your kid put words to feelings.

5. THERE'S NO "U" IN SEX ED. If you feel like you might die of embarrassment just thinking about talking to your son about sex, it's okay. Same goes if you are completely comfy with everything in this chapter and can't wait to dive in with your kid. We're all wired differently and we communicate in unique ways. Just remember that this isn't *your* sex talk, it's *his*. You don't need to download your entire personal history in order to prove vulnerability or coolness or whatever else it is you think you are accomplishing. Tell him a little about your own life if you want, but don't dominate.

6. COVER LEGAL GROUND. As your kid gets older, you really must include topics that span intimacy and legality. These include sexting: both what to do if someone asks you for a nude picture (answer: don't send one!) and why your kid shouldn't solicit a nude from someone else. There's also consent, rape, and the impact of drugs and alcohol, each of which deserves its own conversation, but they also need to be covered together because your son must know that consent doesn't exist in the presence of drugs or alcohol. There's a whole lot more to discuss in the legal bucket, but I don't want to overwhelm you. I have saved it for Chapter 7 . . .

7. DON'T ASSUME THEY KNOW IT ALL. Even if your child's school has a robust curriculum, even if he has watched every episode of *Big Mouth* or has four older siblings, make sure that he knows correct facts about anatomical parts, birth control, and STDs.

8. EMPHASIZE LOVE, NOT FEAR. Don't demonize sex, because the ultimate goal is for your kid to have great sex as part of a loving relationship one day in the future—emphasis for most of you on "future." Remember that if you always frame sex in a negative light, then that day will come when your kid has sex (as almost all humans do) and you have set things up such that he cannot talk to you about it. Not to mention that your negativity about sex today can result in feelings of shame within him later on. So above all, don't forget to discuss love.

Chapter Seven
BOYS AND SEX:
THE GAME-CHANGING ROLES OF
PORN, NUDES, AND CONSENT

WE LIVE IN AN IMAGE-BASED CULTURE barraging us from every direction and playing out on increasingly tiny screens. Pictures, memes, games, GIFs, video shorts, TV shows, full-length features . . . This content is available wherever we are, flowing freely (often literally) across websites, apps, digital platforms, and now more than ever social media. In case that's not enough, there's a second layer of content stacked on top of the first: those ubiquitous ads filling the margins of a web page, popping up to obscure the screen, or maximally blurring the line between paid-for and authentic by simply inserting themselves into a feed as if they are part of the user-generated content. Amid the bombardment in all its shapes and sizes—be it creative or newsy, objective or editorial, purchased or free—these days it's easy to forget that though we actively seek information, it also passively and aggressively solicits us.

Adults do battle with this ever-expanding content monster for sure, yet somehow it feels more ferocious for our kids. Partly that's because we adults have fully mature prefrontal cortices that should, in theory, allow us to choose to put away our devices or at the very least turn off notifications, recognize ads when we see them, and tread cautiously while Googling. But hold any teenager's phone for five minutes, and you'll hear the deluge; in silent mode you'll feel it, and it feels like a completely unsatisfying, stuttering massage. Notifications, likes, and comments light up their limbic systems even more than ours. If that doesn't make sense, go reread Chapter 5.

Thanks to this new normal of content overload, no longer is there a version of sheltering ourselves or our connected kids from anything: shootings or natural disasters; political dramas; bikini selfies; the Kardashians; that coveted sweater going on sale; or porn. Especially porn.

Did that last one surprise you? It shouldn't, because porn is everywhere. Maybe you've noticed. If you haven't, just open your eyes a little bit wider the next time you scroll and you'll start to see it—while hardcore is generally relegated to X-rated websites that are just a click away, softer-core images run rampant, from professionally produced ads to selfie nudes snapped on phones and uploaded to text, social media, and dating apps. "Everywhere" might be an understatement.

Now consider the kid with questions about what the heck is happening to a certain body part, or whether something is "normal." With a phone in hand, he can easily bypass parents, teachers, friends, not to mention the ancient notion of books, on a quest for information. At the tap of his finger appears a picture or, better yet, a video to show him what he wants to know—and often way more than he bargained for—in the privacy of the palm of his hand. This overwhelming image buffet consists of things that most kids don't really want to witness, and none of which they can un-see.

So forget framing a conversation about, literally, anything—from history lessons to social commentary to, yes, porn—in a way that you think might work best for your child, because CNN or BuzzFeed or Instagram or Pornhub are having that talk well before you can, sometimes verbally but more often via images. Today it's foolishness to think that we can curate our kids' entertainment, let alone environment, and this represents a pretty fundamental shift in the experience of being both a parent and a kid. Simply put, they see more than we did when we were their age, even if they aren't really looking for it. Especially porn.

This issue is gender-neutral . . . but it's not. Pornographic images can be seen by males and females equally, but in the world of adolescents, boys tend to seek them out more often. This is not to say that our daughters aren't impacted—they are, and how!—but it's important to understand why boys in their teens, and even tweens, tend to find themselves trapped in pornography's web. The data is murky here, but almost everyone who studies the subject seems to agree that while porn is extending its reach to younger and younger audiences, grabbing an increasing number of eyeballs, it's the males who struggle most with porn addiction—or at least repetitive viewing.

The goal of this chapter is not to scare you. Rather, it is to open your eyes to a new world order and provide you the tools to raise your son within it; or, if he is already pretty much grown, to reorient your conversations with a hefty dose of reality. Because current studies suggest that upward of 90% of boys eighteen and younger have seen porn; for girls, it's 60%. I don't like thinking about this stuff any more than you do, but they're watching whether or not we talk to them about it, and it looks nothing like a 1970s magazine centerfold. Gone is even the hint of intimacy or seduction, let alone a finite number of pages to view. Instead there exists a parade of videos showing people (one, two, often many more) engaging in frank sex, generally aggressive, often cloaked in violence. Stories of sex that don't just lack romance, they lack consent. As soon as the first clip ends, another is ready to be viewed—or maybe it starts playing automatically—and after that another, and then another. The images our kids see imprint on them, almost always without us parents ever knowing it. That these sometimes ethically abhorrent, not to mention illegal, dynamics play out on the very same screens that display family vacation photos and *Words with Friends* is mind-boggling.

Add all of this together, and we parents have a decision to make: we can talk about this stuff sooner than we might want, or we can outsource the conversation to the image-based content machines we bought our kids so that they could text us from middle school. Either way, we cannot spare our children today's ubiquitous graphic sexual content. But if we start talking about it, we stand a chance of minimizing their exposure, anticipating what they will undoubtedly encounter, communicating the dire consequences of such behavior in real life, and ultimately shifting the lens through which they view it all.

THE DOMINATION OF PORN CULTURE

In October 2016, I sat in a crowded San Francisco convention center ballroom, pediatricians as far as the eye could see, at the plenary session for the American Academy of Pediatrics (AAP) annual meeting. If you've never been to an academic meeting, the plenary is the general assembly. Anywhere else it would be called the keynote, but that's academia for you.

I vaguely recall one of the speakers mentioning that 10,000 pediatricians had registered for the conference that year. I have no idea how many of them were in the room, but I wouldn't be surprised if it was close to that number. Packed, I tell you. A great place to have pretty much any pediatric emergency.

The plenary offers a slate of speakers, including one star who consumes the biggest chunk of time. In 2016 the show starred Gail Dines, even though most people in the room had never heard of her before. Gail is a professor of sociology and women's studies at Wheelock College in Boston and, above all else, an expert on pornography. She loves to disarm the audience by introducing herself as a Boston local. "Cawn't you hear it?" she asks in what is actually a thick British accent. Really what she's saying is, *Don't worry, there will be moments of laughter,* which is a relief because the next thing out of her mouth is how she's going to walk us through the highly sexualized—"pornified," she calls it—landscape where our kids live. That's not so funny.

Gail delivered her jaw-dropping forty-five-minute talk to a group of professionals on the frontlines of children's health, and as she did, the faces of the elder statesmen drained to match the shocks of white hair on their heads. Most of us—myself included—were largely clueless about current-day porn.

You see, while pediatricians are trained to ask our patients about sexual activity, educate them about STDs, and cover issues like sexual identity, physical safety, and pregnancy prevention, the vast majority of us still equated pornography with sneaking a peek at your dad's *Playboy*. And, frankly, we almost never brought it up in the office. First of all, who had the time? There was so much to cover (nutrition, exercise, sleep, hygiene, helmets, sunscreen, seatbelts, and screen time, just to start) before getting to sex (which requires talking through physical logistics, emotional repercussions, and biological consequences like pregnancy and disease transmission)—how were we expected to add porn into that fifteen-minute visit? But secondly, and perhaps more profoundly, we didn't cover porn in the checkup checklist because why would we? This, to the best of our collective knowledge, wasn't a particularly significant pediatric health issue.

Gail disabused us of that notion and then some. It's a major issue, she argued, one that affects both our boys and our girls, albeit in radically different directions.

Gail explained in vivid detail the dominance of pornography online, sharing staggering statistics like: 35% of all Internet downloads are pornographic; 40 million Americans are regular visitors to porn sites, with 70% of all men (boys, really) ages eighteen to twenty-four on these sites in a typical month; and 25% of all search engine requests are pornography-related. Dizzy yet? The data has grown ever more overwhelming in the past few years since I first heard Gail speak at the plenary. By the end of 2018, Pornhub, the most dominant porn site on the

Web (and, worth noting, part of the larger umbrella company MindGeek, the largest pornography clearinghouse in the world) drew an average of 92 million visitors per day. If you think you know what your kid is up to—especially if you are reading this while running the thread *not my son* through the back of your mind—take note that recent research estimates that half of all eleven-year-old boys have seen online porn, though the better data suggests the average age of first viewing is more like twelve or thirteen. Whether it's happening to your son in sixth, seventh, or eighth grade, researchers clearly agree that by the end of middle school the majority of boys have been porn-exposed. We parents, meanwhile, remain woefully naive: only half of us with porn-watching kids between fourteen and eighteen are aware of what they are actually viewing on their laptops and phones. And when parents are asked about specific sexual encounters our kids are witnessing, we underestimate their viewing habits by as much as tenfold.*

From the stage at the AAP conference, Gail went on to describe the broad range of what kids see when they stumble upon online porn: everything from hypersexualized snapshots to cringeworthy videos playing out sex-meets-violence fantasies. There are story lines (or at least camera lenses) focused on guys, for sure, but the vast majority spotlight women. Some of this content is professionally produced, but in recent years a

---

* Of course, middle school girls are exposed to pornography in huge numbers too. But the data is more muddled here. At the moment, most studies suggest that boys are first to see porn, so if the average first viewing for boys is during middle school, then the average first viewing for girls is, presumably, later.

Some of the most stunning data is published by the pornography sites themselves. I cannot get enough of Pornhub's self-published statistics, which reside on their website—but fully separate from any pornographic images—under the banner "Year in Review." It's like their annual report, beaming with pride. One highlight from the 2017 summary included the following stat: In 2017, a total of 595,482 hours of video were uploaded, which is sixty-eight *years* of porn if watched continuously.

disconcerting (and ever-growing) chunk is made by amateurs on cellphones, accounting for the dramatic rise in content volume. And while these still photos and videos are equally available to females and males, over time it's the males who stay tuned.

Since a side effect of watching a lot of porn is the need for increasingly stimulating imagery in order to achieve orgasm—and Gail was blunt here: orgasm is the goal for most porn watchers, at least the seasoned ones—over the past decade or so, pornographers have felt compelled to go beyond filming just body parts and the interaction of those parts. They have ratcheted things up by tethering sex to violence, a move clearly directed at male viewers.* I didn't find this terribly surprising, actually, given our broader cultural shift toward mainstreaming all sorts of content that would have been shunned, censored, or both in a nanosecond when we were coming of age. Remember the 1980s definition of an R-rated movie, not to mention the guy sitting in the ticket booth checking for age verification? Ah, how things have changed. As a result of this pendulum swing, today there's a new normal not just in the abundance of easy-access porn on mobile devices, but also in its intensity and aggressiveness, almost always directed against females. Because content creators fight for eyeballs, and everyone has access to essentially everything online, we are bound to see increasingly outrageous images. And we do. And so do our kids.

This escalation isn't confined to a virtual vacuum—it has

---

* A friend of mine—male, not that it matters—read this sentence and found it offensive. I get his reaction, but I disagree, which is why I left it in. While violent imagery draws in female viewers across platforms like film, TV, and video games, we know that it draws in male viewers more. Further, while I am sure there are some women in the world who may claim to enjoy watching porn with sexual violence perpetrated against women, there is absolutely no doubt that these women are few and far between. And so, while I deeply appreciate that there are many men out there who find sexual violence reprehensible—and I am grateful for this—it still stands that the escalation of these "story lines" was meant to draw in male viewers.

consequences that impact real life. Gail focused most on erectile dysfunction, also known as E.D., a term familiar to anyone who has watched a television commercial break at any point over the last handful of years. Multiple studies show that males who watch porn regularly and then attempt sex in real life experience much higher rates of E.D. Why? Because actual sex is boring by comparison. And we're not just talking about adult men here. Some data on teenage porn viewers shows a similarly increasing incidence of E.D., which is kind of amazing when you stop and think about it, given the stereotype of the adolescent male who is always up for sex—these days, there's a distinction between being up for it and *up* for it. In decades past, E.D. was a rare diagnosis before middle age and usually written off to hormonal imbalance or prostate issues, but it seems this may no longer be the case, thanks to the evolution of porn.

Another side effect of widely available porn in its current iteration is the redefinition of what sexual partners are looking for. As porn has evolved, its standard story line revolves around—or at least climaxes with—increasingly aggressive degradation of women. Gail's examples included strangulation and suffocation, many-on-one sex (often gang rape), and forceful anal sex. These tropes appear so frequently in porn that they no longer represent extremes. An almost palpable wave of nausea passed through the crowd as we all had a moment to consider how we counsel kids in our practices. While we certainly cover safety in relationships, I for one had never thought I needed to tell a girl—or a boy, for that matter—that strangulation isn't okay, or that the choice to have sex doesn't imply consent to anal.

Before Gail left the stage, she widened her scope. There are plenty of kids, she explained, who haven't been exposed to hardcore pornographic imagery, boys and girls alike. And even with the ubiquity of it all, many will never stumble into the worst of it. Cue the collective sigh. But, Gail argued, the new normal doesn't just apply to the extremes. Our culture has reset the meter of acceptability when it comes to sexualized images in general, a phenomenon that accelerated when celebrities started circulating sex tapes a couple of decades ago. Fast-forward to the current-day practice of trading nude selfies, standard fare at all ages (yes, go ask your single thirty-, forty-, even fifty-something friends who are on dating apps). Even clothed images feel overtly sexual these days, like when middle schoolers pose with their tongues out—not stuck out in that *nah-nah* kind of way, but in that *I'm going to lick something I shouldn't* kind of way. Some of them are so young, they cannot possibly understand the messages they are sending.

Let's be clear: neither Gail's words from that stage nor my interpretation of them from the audience constitutes an anti-sex rant. Rather, both are acknowledgment that our kids are not immune to the sexualization of everything around them; and it filters down, informing the way they present themselves in the world. It's what they see—online and in real life—constantly. Accessible, intensified porn has played a role in the normalization of a hypersexualized mainstream culture, which in turn has pushed porn to further extremes, and so on, à la the chicken and the egg.

I walked out of the session alongside a group of fellow pediatricians, all shell-shocked. It was lunchtime, but no one had an appetite. How had we all missed this? Was Gail overstating the proportions of this epidemic? Or was it playing out right under our noses, and at the same time beyond our lines of sight? Those forty-five minutes marked a point of inflection for so many of the health care providers in that room; mine was a point of no return. As my kids can attest, middle schoolers themselves at the time, after hearing Gail speak, the fact of twenty-first-century porn suddenly consumed me.

I had so many questions, I didn't know where to begin. And so I started with an informal local survey. I began asking kids—patients from my practice, kids in classrooms where I teach, my own children's friends, too (yes, I did that! But they were surprisingly eager to talk, as if they felt relief that someone was asking)—about their exposure to porn, only to discover that they had almost all seen it in one form or another by the time they hit their teens. Some swapped selfie nudes with friends, others were looking at complete strangers; most steered clear of Pornhub and similar sites, but some headed straight to them, and all knew they existed. Their experiences with sexual imagery varied, but each one, in his or her own way, described porn as a side effect of connectivity as a way of life. With parents gifting their kids smartphones at increasingly young ages, and schools requiring an Internet connection to complete homework assignments, all of our kids are online exploring around the clock and inevitably lots of them—maybe most, males and females, the ones who are sexually active and those who have never had sex, nor even an image of what sex will be for them—stumble onto the naked spectrum with super-sexual imagery at one end and hardcore porn at the other. Just as Gail had said.

And mind you, I don't expect that everyone disclosed the full truth to me. These conversations are awkward, embarrassing, and vulnerable. I am used to talking to kids directly—I was trained to do it as a pediatrician, and it is probably my favorite part of the job—but even so, this line of questioning presents a big ask. The fact that nearly every one of them described at least some porn exposure speaks volumes; when underreporting is factored in, that volume becomes almost deafening.

I wanted to understand how kids found their way there and if this younger set, the tweens and teens and college kids, were mainly male. In short, yes, but it's not quite so simple. A handful of the kids I spoke with—both boys and girls—acknowledged actively looking for porn, but most told me that porn actually found them. It happened often, particularly when they were searching for an answer to an unrelated question, maybe to define a word or understand what the heck was happening to a specific body part; for a few, it was while looking to bust a newfound "fact" as urban myth. And then there were the kids who weren't asking about any of this—they just accidentally slipped up with a typo in the search bar, or clicked on an ad, or discovered a nude photo in a text thread or instant message. Regard-less of the path, *wham!*—they were staring at porn. This process of discovery was fairly gender-neutral.

In fact, when I asked them the question *How many kids have seen porn by the time they reach the end of their teens?*, my interviewees uniformly answered, *Basically everyone*. The published data is a little less dramatic—the highest number I can find in an actual study suggests that upward of 80% of all girls under twenty have seen porn, and 97% of all boys. Still, this isn't statistically far from "everyone." Interestingly, though, they're not all watching. There's a big difference between seeing porn once and regularly viewing it, one that many studies don't distinguish. The research that does look at this suggests there's a huge gender difference when it comes to routine watching. In one study, for instance, only 8% of girls found it impossible to turn off porn and walk away from the screen, while nearly three times as many boys (23%) said the same.

THE GENDER DIVIDE

This asymmetry between boys' and girls' experience shook me. Girls seemed to have resilience to porn, describing an ability to see it but move on, while boys often found themselves pulled in, watching for longer or revisiting the sites again another time. Let me be clear about this gender divide: It's not that the girls didn't find porn just as readily as the boys, clearly they did; it's not that some girls didn't seek it out, they did that too; and it's not that porn doesn't affect them, of course it does. Porn just seems to impact girls and boys differently, at least according to my very nonscientific, heavily anecdotal survey of kids living in a small corner of Southern California, plus a few small published studies. Psychologists often describe a pattern of returning to the site of an unhealed trauma, and while the boys I spoke with returned over and over again, the girls by-and-large told me that they didn't. This suggests to me that for girls, the trauma of porn could be otherwise managed. And trust me, I fully get it that this isn't always the case.

My study of a thoroughly non-random sample of kids is not meant to parade as science, and it's entirely possible that the girls I spoke to grossly underreported their experiences or their interest in porn. Maybe they were just telling me what they thought I wanted to hear. But I think their comments tell a story that makes sense: the reason for the gender difference in young porn viewing might just boil down to talking about it. Every single female I asked described growing up in a culture that encourages conversations, beginning with body talk in their early tweens when they first experienced their own curves. Most girls told me that because information is readily available to them and conversation is encouraged at every turn, they feel comfortable wondering aloud about anything body-related, they use anatomically correct language, and they ask questions free of shame. They credit this cultural approach to puberty with steering them away from porn when it appears—they don't need to seek out answers in isolation, and they don't buy the narrative of woman as victim or sex slave or punching bag that porn so often sells.* Without realizing it, these girls were making the case for conversation as a key ingredient of resilience.

These girls are not entirely immune to the effects of porn, though, because a significant number of them do wind up online watching: studies show that teenage girls are much more likely to do this than women in their mid-twenties. More than that, as all of these girls—both the watchers and the non-watchers—become sexually active, they are highly aware of the influence of porn on the dynamics of intimacy (including ex-

---

* Restating here for emphasis: clearly this is not the case for all women. There are endless examples of the opposite—victimized women who give over to the narrative, and victimizing men who impose it. I just find it fascinating that talking about body changes may provide fertile soil for the roots of a movement that one day, hopefully, will disrupt this pattern.

pectations around anal sex, bondage, having males ejaculate on them, filming the sex; I could go on . . .), and many describe giving over to them. But what these budding women *don't* describe, at least among my small sampling plus the girls queried in the few official studies on this topic, too, is a routine of watching porn incessantly.

In contrast sit the boys, who do seem to watch porn—at least more often—and who are not socialized to talk about it. Neither, by the way, are their parents. The world expects them to go quiet (how many times have you heard a parent bemoan: *I have a teenage boy, so of course I know nothing about his life*), and many of us reinforce the silence when it happens. This is exacerbated by the fact that the first couple of years of boys' puberty is generally spent not knowing they are in it. The chattier tween girls become, the quieter their male counterparts. Not all, but stereotypes often exist for a reason. The boys I surveyed agreed wholeheartedly with this generalization, most doing so with a nod or a simple "Yep."

Here's my damning math, which adds up to a boy porn problem: the average age for a boy to start surging testosterone and tip into puberty is ten (nine if he's black); likewise, the average age for an American child to get a smartphone, or other mobile digital device that is deemed "theirs," is also ten. With testicles slowly growing come novel experiences (wet dreams!) and feelings (early sexual attraction!) that are bound to confuse even the smartest among them. It's the perfect setup: *Got questions? Ask Google.* And that's how many of the boys I spoke with described their inadvertent introduction to porn. *Click here for the answer to the question you cannot possibly ask aloud, or the one you never knew you had.*

In my own mini-investigation, almost every kid, regardless of gender, mentioned the ease of access to pornography thanks to Google with its warp speed and endless results list, but they gave specific credit to the uber-efficient Google Images search option. In this screen, results pop up in a photo array. Why would anyone opt for a search that spits back words and provides only a handful of links per page (links to more words), every single one of these kids explained to me, when I can trade that for dozens of images fast-tracked to get me where I think I want to go? That's the difference between a Google search and a Google Images search. And by the way, adults, if you haven't tried this when you are researching counter stools or value packs of batteries or how to remove bloodstains, you really should—our kids are onto something. Also, if you haven't discovered this yet, you are at least a decade behind the curve. Google, of course, isn't the only path to porn. Kids point to YouTube's infamous recommended videos that pop up in the page margin, Snapchat's slate of ads, Instagram's sponsored content, and dozens (though the real number is likely hundreds) of other versions of "we search for you" engines producing menus filled with highly sexualized imagery a click away. All of these different ways to be bombarded with graphic images and overwhelming information, and all of which my interviewees had experienced firsthand, many regularly.

The thesis of this entire book is that puberty radically changes how our kids talk to us and how we talk to them, and this shift empowers the communicators (who are more often girls) while leaving the non-communicators (typically the boys) at a distinct disadvantage. This gender difference in conversational comfort may just be the lynchpin when it comes to managing the impact of pornography, because the ones who describe an innate comfort with body talk—the girls—are the same ones who seem to be able to turn the porn off. Maybe they don't need porn's "education," because they have enough good resources readily available. Maybe they see it and share what they've seen with someone who debunks the mythical story lines. There are a dozen reasons I could come up with to explain why girls seem to be more resilient here—someone needs to do that study!— but I am willing to bet it has everything to do with open lines of communication.

THE KID/PARENT DIVIDE

After my exposure to Gail and my conversations with tweens, teens, and college kids, I felt like an idiot given the major boat I had missed. To spare other parents the same sense of inadequacy, I started to share my intel with them. All but a few looked at me sideways.

Parents don't entirely believe this story of easy-access porn, because we are online all day and night too, and we aren't swimming in a sea of nakedness. So how is it possible that's the online universe our kids occupy? But I told them what I (now) knew and passed on this advice: Pay attention to the ads popping up on your screens; slow your scroll and look at the clickbait in your feeds; search a phrase you might have searched when you were younger if there were such an option. We might not click on this stuff—we might not even register that it exists—because we know where it will take us. But our kids? With their surging hormones and newfound feelings of sexual curiosity and famously imbalanced processing of risk versus reward, they're bound to take the bait (which, incidentally, leads them to being baited more often; search engines know what you're looking for and offer it up unsolicited). They're not thinking consequentially. Frankly, even if they are, they may not know where those bread crumbs lead. So they click and land on porn. And then—as many kids have described it to me, at least—they watch. Maybe just for a moment, maybe longer. Maybe a few of them, particularly the boys, go back again and then again, because it's titillating. It's porn, for god's sake! It's a multi-billion dollar online industry (some estimate as much as $97 billion) for a reason.

And therein lies the conundrum: they watch even though they know they aren't supposed to, and it turns them on (particularly the boys) even if it's a little bit aggressive or scary or gross or too much too soon. Here are born feelings of embarrassment quickly morphing to shame, and as most of the boys I queried explained, they didn't know how they could possibly talk to a parent or even a friend about any of this when they stumbled across it . . . and they all stumble across some form of it.

I can no longer count the number of calls I have received over the years that start with *Oh my God, you were right*.

The more I learned, the more it fueled my anger. Because none of this is accidental. The collective porn industry isn't targeting middle-aged men and accidentally picking up a few straggler teenage boys along the way. No. There exists a highly lucrative long-term play to engage young viewers. As most everyone knows by now—including the creators and distributors of porn—the developing brains of tweens, teens, and twenty-somethings are more susceptible to stimulation of all sorts. In the most simplistic terms, this is why kids are more likely to become addicted to just about anything (nicotine, gaming, and—surprise, surprise—porn; much more on this in Chapter 9) compared with fully mature adults. So when a website gets young eyeballs, it is slightly more likely to keep those eyeballs coming back over and over again. Most kids don't have much money to spend, and even if they do, they have grown up in a world where free content is king, so the porn industry offers introductory material for free. This standard loss leader business strategy brings viewers in and keeps them watching long enough to prime their brains to crave more—more videos, more intensity, more outlandishness—at which point the sites start to charge.

This is why it's no accident that our kids wind up on porn sites, Gail explained all those years ago, and I completely concur. Not to excuse parents from all culpability when it comes to what kids do on their screens, but if your kid is watching online porn, most of the time that's neither your fault nor his—this recruitment process is a well-oiled and -funded machine designed to draw your son in and keep him there, particularly if he doesn't know how to talk to anyone about what he is seeing.

The primary consequence of growing up in a porn culture is that these images are writing the stories of sex for our children.

They are redefining beauty ideals and sexual expectations. We don't see what they see on their screens, nor do we have any clue how this plays out for our kids when they are alone with a boyfriend, girlfriend, or an fwb (that's "friend with benefits," for the newbies). We are generally clueless when it comes to how they prep for potential sexual encounters (spoiler alert: many of them *fully groom*, which means they completely remove all pubic hair by shaving, waxing, even permanently lasering—porn influence, anyone?). And even if we intellectually understand that porn culture incorporates tremendous aggression and violence, we still tend not to anticipate that our daughters are at increasing risk of abuse, and our sons are under the impression that this is somehow okay, or at the very least an acceptable, mainstream even, component of sex. As porn has shifted in this general direction, and as younger and younger viewers watch, the lesson to them is that sex and violence go together. This has translated into a noticeably higher likelihood that porn-watching females will be on the receiving end of abuse, and porn-watching males are more likely to perpetrate it.

I have never met a parent who doesn't hope that their child will grow up to find a loving, safe relationship. This absolutely includes their kids' future—or current—sex life, even though pressing a parent to say so may make them blush. I say this lest anyone confuse my message: sex-positivity is the goal (for all of us!), but watching porn that tethers sex to pain, suffering, cruelty, or unwillingness does not get us there. Talking about all of this just might.

Unless we talk to them, kids won't know that the stories of sex they see playing out across their screens are fictional. So talk to your kids about porn, whether or not you think they have seen it. There are lots of tips about how to do this at the end of the chapter. The key, though, is to open up the conversation so often that when they do see it, or at least when they are ready to talk about it, they know you are ready to listen.

WHAT NEEDS TO BE SAID WHEN TALKING ABOUT PORN

Some parents worry that they will be judged by others for sharing too much too soon with their kids—other parents worry about the exact opposite. Let go of any fear of judgment and just focus on the goal: informing your kid. Here's a list of topics that need to be addressed in the context of sex. But remember, there's lots of time to do this because these talks should happen repeatedly, many times over many years.

TALK ABOUT SAFETY. Make it clear that violence and aggression have no place in intimacy. Define these terms, because they include a whole lot more than you may initially be thinking.

LEARN ABOUT FEDERAL LAWS COVERING CHILD PORN. They are serious and enforceable. Kids will say that everyone they know has sent or received a nude from another kid, and no one is in jail as a result. While that may be true for them, there are many examples of enforcement that have radically altered the trajectory of a good kid's life. Look up a few online. The stories are powerful. Along these same lines, learn the rules at your son's school. Have conversations about why a school may not want to open a federal case in the midst of a sexting scandal. But they can, and some do . . .

MAKE A PLAN ABOUT WHAT TO DO WHEN HE IS ASKED FOR A NUDE. Someone will almost inevitably request one, so have a plan. Help him find a way of saying no that feels comfortable for him. I have heard of kids who reply to the request by sending a picture of noodles ("noods") or a neutral color palette. Many kids just don't reply, and that's a great strategy too. Make sure he knows that some social media apps promise an image will disappear after it is opened, but the images are not really gone and can be easily screenshot, saved, and forwarded. Most kids are well aware of this fact, but it never hurts to remind them.

MAKE A PLAN ABOUT WHAT TO DO WHEN HE RECEIVES A NUDE. This one is fairly inevitable as well. The best plan is to delete immediately. I have always told my kids that they can absolutely show me if I am around, but possession of child porn is a crime, so the longer they keep it on their phone the longer they risk being caught with it. In other words, I don't need to see the nude to believe they received it. Make a major point of reminding him (over and over again) that he can never forward the image.

DISCUSS ERECTILE DYSFUNCTION. It's a thing these days. If hardcore porn is required for orgasm, your son may have difficulty getting or maintaining an erection during sex, a situation described to me by boys as scary on the one hand and humiliating on the other. If you share the facts, he is more likely to talk to you if this happens or tell you that it has. And if you feel overwhelmed, there are several excellent online resources on the topic, or you can reach out to your pediatrician for help.

NUDES AND PERSONAL PORN

That was a hefty dose of porn, and I am sure you are hoping this chapter will wrap up just about now. But not so fast. Thankfully, because we all need a silver lining, there is some good news to report: a huge number of kids bypass the porn industry's bait. If, depending upon which study you believe, half of all eleven- or twelve- or thirteen-year-old boys see porn, that means half don't. There's also a tremendous difference between kids who stumble upon it once and frequent watchers, even though the studies don't always do the best job of distinguishing between those groups. This is not to downplay the issue, but it's important to contextualize it: while porn-exposure numbers are alarming, chronically watching strangers go at it is not an inevitable rite of passage.

Unfortunately, that's not the end of the porn story. These kids that bypass Pornhub and its X-rated cousins aren't entirely insulated. In fact, there's a whole wide world of alternate imagery to contend with completely outside of hardcore porn: user-generated nudes. And, it turns out, the culture of swapping naked pictures is far more pervasive than watching X-rated videos, particularly among kids. Since Pornhub alone claims more than 92 million daily viewers, that's saying something.

Don't believe me? Then ask your kid what I asked dozens and dozens of them: *Have you ever sent or received nude images? Has someone asked you for one, or have you been the asker? How about your friends or siblings, have they been asked or done the asking?* Nearly 100% of the kids I queried—and these are questions I have asked for years now and continue to ask in every single class I teach on the subject—say that by the time of middle school graduation, they had been solicited for or the recipient of nudes, noodz, noods, nudz . . . there are so many creative spellings.* Even in sixth-grade classes, I get a unanimous yes,

---

* Nudes are a whole lot like sexting, which technically translates to *sex + texting*. But since sexting implies the use of text, I opt for the term "nudes," which can be sent across text for sure but tend to be shared over a wide range of social media platforms. Kids choose this term, as well, by the way. And since they are growing up in a highly visual culture, it makes sense. But it feels important to remind them that, just as there are implications to sending nude

though in this age demographic most of them just know someone who has been asked but they themselves haven't been solicited. Still, was that what you were grappling with when you
were twelve? Were you waiting to become a teenager, anticipating being asked to share a topless or bottomless photo?

Nudes are a far cry from Pornhub porn, but they represent
a different version, another consequence, of the hyper-
sexualization of our world—just in a totally different direction.
Your kids can name a wide range of folks sending nude images
out into the universe, from role models to other kids at school
(just ask them), and this pushes some of the rest of them to do
the same. Here's the catch: while adults in our society are free
to swap images of themselves and derive what they want from
that—fame, fortune, or just a fleeting moment of attention—
kids aren't. Any naked image of a person under the age of eighteen is child pornography, a federal crime. That's true even if
the picture was taken volitionally, even if it's a selfie snapped
uncoerced and shared willingly. Doesn't matter—it's child porn.
So when the culture encourages kids to do it (both girls and
boys alike, don't be fooled), there can be serious consequences.
Let's say a girl likes a boy and that boy asks her to send a nude,
a surprisingly common request during the flirting stage. When
she snaps a pic, she has produced child porn. When she texts
the image to him, she has distributed child porn. And when she
uploads the nude he sent in return, she's in possession of child
porn. That's three different crimes.

The laws were initially established to protect kids from adult
child-predators, blockading child pornographers and sex traf-
fickers, but they have backfired. Today, thanks to cameras inside every phone plus texting—or better yet, social media apps,
especially the ones that promise messages will disappear—some
of the most common offenders are the kids themselves. The

---

images, so too are there ramifications of sharing sexual content in the form of
words.

issue of nude selfie swaps is so massive, it could occupy an entire book. Maybe next time. But because it's a natural extension of porn—its own form, really—there's no way to write this chapter without including it. So for now I am going to do so with brevity, skipping most of the legal issues and focusing on the social consequences instead.

Female nudes are usually quick snaps of the top half, since the general goal is to get the boobs in the frame. Some girls send full-body shots, but many younger ones especially will lift their shirt, hold a phone in front of them, click, upload, and send, all in thirty seconds or less, no editing required. Many of them don't particularly care how they look, a fact that I find tremendously ironic but is evidenced by the vast majority of the images they send through social media apps like Snapchat every day (a kneecap, the ceiling, a scrunched-up face, often blurry). The point is that much of the time, nudes are taken quickly and impulsively—at least when it's tweens and teens taking the photos—and girls aren't thinking about how identifying features like their lips, chin, neck, freckles, hair color, and jewelry might appear as well. This might feel like no big deal if you are sending the image to someone who really likes you (parents will generally disagree), but it's a *very* big deal when that person forwards it along to others (kids and parents tend to be on the same page here). Not all of the time, but a fair amount of the time, the girl in the nude can be named.

Compare this to boy nude selfies, aka dick pics. Same swiftness, same impetuous upload. The big difference is that the guys are pulling down their pants and taking a picture from a bird's-eye view. Not always, mind you, but much of the time. So there really are no identifying features in this frame—maybe you'll see legs and feet, perhaps even the lower belly, but how often can you look at a snapshot involving the bottom half of the body and say definitively, *Yeah! That's Jimmy from math class!*

The currency of swapping nudes is enormous, with kids participating in numbers that boggle the mind. The consequences are quite different, though, for boys and girls. Any nude can be forwarded, and many are. Because the girls don't always maintain anonymity here, this can be socially devastating; meanwhile, boys who remain unidentified are slightly untouchable. This might read like an upside for boys, as if something in this chapter is finally going their way. But I don't see it like that. In fact, it feels as if the anonymity of their nudes reinforces for boys a lack of consequences . . . that is, until there are some. In other words, there is a downside to the fact that boys face fewer downsides to sending naked images of themselves: it increases the likelihood that they will participate. It's the rare kid who turns down an endorphin rush when there are no consistent repercussions. Meanwhile, spend five minutes researching this topic and you'll find stories of kids expelled from school, others stripped of scholarships, and some even facing prosecution, all because of nudes on their phones. The girls are more likely to pay the social penalty for appearing in the pictures (though boys also can, for sure); the boys to face consequences of possession, distribution, sometimes even selling (though this happens to girls, too). Both sides of the equation are dark.

I have come to believe that among adolescents, the impact of nude swapping is as profound as that of hardcore porn; in some ways it may even be greater. Beyond the legal issues, nudes are personal, they tether to reputation, and they can be used to bully and extort. Nudes don't just plant a visual seed of what sex might be like, they also introduce an individual's expression of sexuality and project that to the wider world, all the while breaking the law.

There's a reason I dumped two high-intensity topics on you at once in a single chapter—and by the way, let me congratulate you for making it this far (you're almost done!), because either one of these issues, hardcore porn or nude swapping, is intense enough to make you want to quit parenting or this book, possibly both. But they are as important as they are bile-inducing, and they share a critical common theme: consent.

HOW TO PREVENT PORN EXPOSURE IN THE FIRST PLACE

If I had the answer, I wouldn't have needed to write this chapter in the first place. But there are two ways of minimizing it, both underutilized.

First, GET DEVICES OUT OF THE BEDROOM AT NIGHT. Did you feel like I yelled that? Good. Pediatricians have preached this for years, usually pointing out that kids sleep more when their devices are separated from them. But the data on porn is equally compelling. The later it gets, the more likely kids are to be online watching porn or swapping nudes. It's not that these activities can't happen at noon, but they are far more likely at midnight. Being alone in a bedroom, feeling the privacy of the moment and the impulsivity that tends to grow at night . . . you see where this is going. So, get into a habit of charging all devices—phones, laptops, iPads, whatever—in a common area of the house that's outside of the bedroom. After a while, kids tell me they love this solution because it gives them a forced break from their devices for which they can blame you.

And second, START TALKING ABOUT PORN. In case you missed it, that was the entire point of this chapter. Talking about it protects our kids from seeking it out and helps them manage what they see. It allows them to turn to us in order to process the images they are viewing. It helps us understand what they face in the world, which differs radically from the forces at play when we were growing up. When in doubt, start talking. And listening.

THE COMMON DENOMINATOR OF CONSENT

Consent used to imply agreement, as in *Yeah, that's what I want to do with you in bed (or on the couch or in the back seat of the car or wherever)*. More specifically, for a long time the notion of consent was that "no means no" but everything else means yes. For a hundred reasons, all absurdly obvious in hindsight, this wasn't a great standard. Today, the goal of consent is enthusiastic agreement to a sexual act. *Yes! I do want to do exactly this thing we are doing right this moment!*

Adding to the confusion: though the notion of consent has grown stricter over time, its interpretation varies depending upon where you live, or actually where you have a sexual encounter—which may or may not involve intercourse. Every state has its own definition of consent—there isn't a single nationwide rule. Technically, this means that while one state might deem it okay for a person to touch another person in a certain circumstance and a certain way, the neighboring state might not.

Many college campuses have tried to solve the confusion by imposing their own, generally more stringent rules on this issue. Their version is called *affirmative consent*—sometimes nicknamed Yes Means Yes—and in its strictest interpretation, every single sexual act within an act must be agreed upon. *Yes, you may touch my right shoulder. Now, yes, you may touch my left shoulder. Yes, we can kiss.* Affirmative consent has generated tremendous debate, with parents pitted against one another, siding-up based upon which kid receives the benefit of the doubt in a given case. Regardless of where you may land on the fairness of this particular standard, affirmative consent directly impacts only a limited group of older teens and young twenty-somethings enrolled in college and touching one another in the flesh. It doesn't apply to screen-based activities, only to real-life ones.

None of these versions of consent tackle stranger porn or naked selfie swaps, two radically different but mainstream sexual experiences that begin years before college and often send the singular message that consent is secondary. In hardcore porn, consent is breached if one actor is forced to do something he or she doesn't want to do (tough to prove, if they are being paid) or when the story line portrays him or her as being forced (which isn't a technical violation of consent, but clearly sends a message to viewers that lack of consent is okay—sexy, even). With nudes, it is violated when an image is shared without permission. Nude sharing might seem like a lesser offense, but it's not, it's just a different version, and an insanely common one at that. I challenge you to try to find a school district in the country that hasn't wrestled with a sexting scandal. There is deep significance to this: the norm of both porn viewing and nude exchanges in middle and high school suggests to kids that consent has a very fuzzy definition.

TEACHING CONSENT

If we teach our boys (and our girls) about consent early on, in nonsexual settings, the lessons are even more deeply ingrained when they eventually become intimate with others. This approach adds years onto the front end of consent teaching, which creates deeper muscle memory. Some tips:

MAKE CONSENT ABOUT RESPECTING PEOPLE'S BOUNDARIES, not just their bodies. Man or woman, boy or girl, you wouldn't just take someone's jacket without asking to borrow it—same concept here.

POINT OUT POWER STRUCTURES at your workplace, in school social groups, in politics. Introduce the idea that if a person has power over another person, consent becomes complicated. Saying yes or no is deeply intertwined with free will.

ERR ON THE SIDE OF CAUTION. When in doubt, don't do or say something that might be interpreted as an act of aggression. That advice applies to both us and our kids.

So, what is or isn't okay in the world of sex and sexual expression? And should it matter *where* one has a sexual experience—whether it happens in a particular state or on a college campus, or how about on a screen? Should certain rules shift at age eighteen? Should kids younger than that face prosecution under child pornography laws that were written with them in mind as the victims, not the perpetrators? And where does the Internet stand in all of this? Should porn sites be accountable for restricting underage viewers? (Okay, here I am just going to say it: YES!) Should they be allowed to store and stream content depicting violent and criminal acts? What about search engines and social media sites? Where does free expression end and an acknowledgment of dangerous modeling begin?

I promise, the information dump is over now. But you see why I needed to take you through all of it, right? Because if our job as parents is to keep our kids safe and healthy, then we have to understand the forces in the world that work counter to that job. Porn in all of its iterations, from naked selfies to hardcore films, models a range of behaviors that can put our kids at risk physically, socially, legally, and emotionally. This gigantic topic that was never supposed to be a significant component of parenting has arrived.

Because puberty is both independent of sex and at the same time inextricably linked to it, the playbook about how to approach the enormous topic of sex in general—at home, at school, even in health care settings—is muddled at best. Porn throws a whole new wrench in here, especially because it's as violent and graphic as it is easy to find. A handful of years ago it would have felt absurd to be writing about middle schoolers and porn, but here we are.

This X-rated situation has created a mandate for parents to arm ourselves with information, stay current, and start talking. We are decent at communicating with our girls about these various facets of sex, but we can be better. We are dismal by comparison at talking to our boys about all of it: sex, porn, consent, safety, and the fallacy of what they almost all see on their screens. If we don't open lines of communication here, they risk becoming the ultimate victims of consent confusion: primed to break the law or another person's spirit.

HOW TO TALK TO BOYS ABOUT . . . PORN

There is no gold standard for how to talk about porn, mostly because this is an ever-changing landscape. But if you don't start talking, a chorus of other voices will, among them other kids with deep misconceptions and porn stars modeling the opposite of safe, loving relationships. Plus, our kids face rules about intimacy, pornography, and consent, rules that compete directly with what they see on their screens. So get started.

1. JUST START TALKING ABOUT IT. I am a big believer that it's never too soon to open up conversations about any of this stuff. But at the very least, if your son has access to a mobile device or computer with Wi-Fi, then ideally you should start talking about what to do before he sees sexual imagery. That means if he's six or seven and you are thinking, *He's way too young for that conversation!*, well then maybe you should also

rethink giving him unfettered Internet access at that age, and take back that device.

2. WHAT IF I AM ALREADY LATE TO THE GAME? Even though it's never too early to talk about health and wellness, some parents may feel like they are too late, no matter when they start. So, let me be super clear: it is *never* too late to start talking to your kid about any of this. And if you cannot get beyond that, begin the conversation by saying: *I wish I had brought this up sooner . . .*

3. START THE CONVERSATION WITHOUT JUDGMENT. You can explain that you've read about kids watching porn—that by the end of middle school more than half of boys have seen some, and by the end of high school it's almost all kids, guys and girls—and so you won't be upset if he has. Make yourself available to talk about what he's seen and answer any questions he may have anytime he's ready to talk. Then keep offering regularly until he takes you up on it. And make sure to add that the reason this is so important is that the sex he may have seen online is likely very different from the sex he will one day have. There are a zillion versions of this—do what works for you and your son. But remember: NO judgment and NO shaming. That's the key.

4. PACE YOURSELF. Feel free to open up the floodgates but let the conversation trickle. One way to do that is to start a dialogue and then zip your lip and just wait for him to talk. Ask open-ended questions instead of ones that land at yes/no. The silence can feel unbearable. But sometimes in an effort to get something over with, or even just to get the information across, we do all the talking, dumping it on our kids and giving too much too soon. Watch for signs like shutting down, rolling eyes, walking out of the room . . . they generally aren't very subtle. And remember that you have years of awkward and uncomfortable conversations ahead of you—this topic is not one-and-done!—so you can save some of your enthusiasm for the future.

5. USE ANATOMICAL WORDS! There is nothing wrong with saying *penis* or *testicles* or *anus*. In fact, if you fear those words, you may inadvertently create colossal confusion in an attempt to avoid them. They are not "bad" words. And on that subject, I do think kids should know slang words too. More important, they should know when not to use them and why. Conversations about language and respect can easily go hand in hand.

Chapter Eight
BOYS AND BODY IMAGE:
NO PAIN, NO GAIN

THERE'S A PRETTY POPULAR OUTDOOR MALL near my house in Los Angeles, inhabited by all the stores you would expect. One stretch includes Urban Outfitters, Brandy Melville, Victoria's Secret, a couple of shoe outfits (running shoes, skateboarding shoes, basketball shoes, not a loafer in sight), a store that doubles as a candy mecca . . . it's the block meant to draw in middle and high schoolers. It's also the time- and money-sucking block every parent comes to dread.

I have this very vivid memory of strolling through the mall when my daughter was in fourth grade. It was Christmastime, and we wrapped ourselves in heavy jackets to brave the 60-degree weather, frigid by L.A. standards. As we entered the stretch of aspirational shops selling clothes that wouldn't fit her for at least another couple of years, my daughter stopped in her tracks. Following her line of sight, my eyes fell upon a mostly naked guy. He couldn't have been much more than eighteen, which was not the first thing I noticed. He wore a Santa's hat and a pair of boxers—maybe they were shorts; it felt like a felony to look—and his muscular arms waved us toward Abercrombie & Fitch while his giant smile sparkled in the sunlight. I felt cold just looking at him, but he seemed completely comfortable.

I remember glancing down at my daughter, recognizing for

the first time that she was aware of another human's sexual draw. My mind leapfrogged to her future adolescent and young adult life, which led me to thoughts about dating and safety and then general objectification of women. I did not, however, think for a moment about my son who, at age eight, stood on the other side of me holding my hand. My mental montage starred my daughter and her future growing up in a world that overvalues women for how they look and often undervalues everything else they bring to the table. I didn't consider the Abercrombie guy's impact upon my son (if not today, then one day) or, frankly, on any of the dozens of boys and men walking past the store. I didn't even wonder how the Abercrombie guy himself experienced the entirety of the situation, which is pretty ironic given that I was staring at a mostly naked dude whose entire job it was to be objectified. In hindsight, I feel like a dolt.

Not long afterward, Abercrombie made headlines as it vowed to remove shirtless live models from its storefronts. The brand also promised to turn down the volume of the music pumping through its stores and reduce the intensity of the cologne-scented shopping experience, all steps aimed, as it turns out, at attracting a slightly older demographic. What Abercrombie never did was to begin a conversation about male bodies and the pressure boys and men might feel to look a certain way. The brand had its moment, and then let the moment go. In hindsight, I hope *they* feel like dolts.

You see, while males tend to be acutely aware of the lengths to which females—and the world at large on behalf of females—will go to achieve a particular look, most aren't at all conscious about how these forces impact them. The biggest myth of the beauty myth is that it is almost exclusively female.

Well, it's time to get woke and put a voice to the realities of boy body image.

Beauty standards impact all of our kids, fueling insecurities across the gender board. While girls have the language to talk about their bodies and the encouragement to go there often, boys, at least on this front, have essentially been rendered mute. Yes, girls are at high risk for body image–related issues like eating disorders. But don't be falsely reassured that boys are not. This chapter is about taking on body image with our boys in the same raw way we approach it with our girls, because it turns out boys are suffering too, oftentimes at rates rivaling their female peers. The catch is that male body goals and their resulting disorders can look very different from female ones. Combined with a culture of silence around the male half of this topic, the boy struggle is easy to miss.

BODY GOALS

With the right care and feeding plus exercise, not to mention sleep, in theory almost everyone could have a healthy, fit bod. But we don't. There are a thousand lifestyle levers contributing to this fact, from food (low quality, high volume, and even higher sugar content) to exercise (not enough) to environment (from personal safety to air quality, with everything in between) to economics (both good food and good health care cost big bucks). I haven't even mentioned genetics or even simple lack of sleep. The list of reasons why someone is shaped a certain way runs long—very, very long—and needs to be addressed point by point. Not here, though. This is a chapter about the adjacent issue of how people see their bodies.

For females, the ideal body type has been pluralized. Today, girls are torn between at least three different versions of perfect: one super skinny, another fit and sporty, and of course the one that's ultra-curvy, buxom, and buttocksome. This triad can send mixed messages, yes, but it also allows more women to qualify as, or at least aspire to be, ideal. That's the upside. The downsides—and there are many—include the fact that all three ideal shapes tend to be unrealistically slim, even the curvy version, which has a teeny waist tucked between full hips and breasts.*

By comparison, the male ideal has remained fairly stagnant. The G.I. Joe doll that my brothers played with in the 1970s looks almost exactly like that guy in front of Abercrombie, at least from the neck down. Yes, there is a skinny chic look for guys now too, and there was a period not long ago in which the Dad Bod was hailed as a goal (though I am not sure I ever heard anyone use the term "ideal" for the generous gut of the Dad Bod). But for all intents and purposes, the archetype of masculine perfection described by sixth-grade boys is nothing new, and it's reinforced all around them in the bodies of professional athletes and celebrities, as well as superheroes and gaming avatars. Also not new: boys don't talk much about it. They see "perfect" specimens everywhere they look, but there isn't any national—or even local—conversation about how these largely unattainable images make boys feel.

The quest for the perfect body begins young—many experts say at least as young as ten, which you know by now is when more than half of them have entered puberty and have their own phones, too. I'm talking both boys and girls here, though the vast majority of research looks at the female half of the population. According to some studies, awareness of who has the best bod begins at six or seven, coincidentally when the most precocious ones start grappling with hormones and screen-sized images of what they are presumably supposed to look like. In fact, the pressure to look perfect can actually be felt absurdly early: before the first day of preschool; even before taking a first step. That's because from day one, our kids are steeped in body

---

* Girl body goals are complicated, which is why countless books, blogs, and shows are dedicated to the topic. But there's a valid argument that with increasing attention paid to the subject, there has been a parallel surge in new definitions of female beauty. For sure, there has been a healthy upswing in girl conversation on the topic over the past several decades.

goals almost wherever their gaze lands: billboards, magazines, books, your screens, my screens . . . So immersed in a beauty standard are they, it's somewhat ridiculous to try to come up with an arbitrary starting point for the impact. Essentially, from the minute our kids come out of the womb, those sweet babies beloved for their squeezable thighs and rolls of skin folds live in a culture that messages them to seek the opposite. Boys and girls alike.

For the most part, girls know all about this. Many—most, even—have been raised to see through the images in front of them. By the time girls hit their teens, despite their culture of swapping bikini selfies (often enhanced with a filter to maximize or minimize features here and there), they are well aware of every fix applied to the visuals they confront all day, every day. They understand the transformative nature of those app-based filters, and of makeup and Photoshop and plastic surgery too.

Guys, though, at least before and during puberty, remain largely clueless about the influence of the ideal physique thrust upon them, despite the fact that male images—and many males themselves—are tweaked in all those same ways. Apps that hide zits, taper waists, and enhance muscles are used by both genders. Hair products and dietary supplements are marketed to both groups too. Even plastic surgery is becoming equal opportunity, with increasing numbers of men opting for things like hair transplants; cheek, butt, or calf implants; and breast reductions. Despite this, our conversations tend to be about female beauty standards set by doctored images (and by literally doctored women). The manipulation of men flies almost completely under the radar, even though it's basically just as common.

Many girls talk about their bodies and how they feel about their bodies and how the world conspires against their authentic selves with its unattainable, unreal female body goals. Most boys don't.

And so when I teach middle schoolers about body image, the conversation is almost always dominated by the girls, comfortable with the topic and hell-bent on opening the boys' eyes to the unfairness of the situation. Within moments of asking boys to chime in, eleven- and twelve-year-old guys—who by the way are all over the puberty spectrum, with some a foot taller and an octave deeper than others—begin to articulate the enormous pressure *they* feel. Many of them say they never even recognized it until the conversation in class at that very moment. The onus of their body goals may be bigger than the burden placed on girls, they explain, because it festers so quietly. Six-pack abs, no hair on the chest, a full head of hair on the head (or a perfectly round, shaved scalp), not a pimple in sight, straight glimmering teeth, broad shoulders, visible biceps, lean but definitely not too thin . . . The number of items on their unrealistic standards tally goes on. Most of the girls have never considered male body pressures; and if the boys have, close to none of them have ever shared their feelings. I watch as the girls listen, their eyes growing wide, dumbfounded by the enumeration of these issues.

SIZE AND SCOPE

Boy body image isn't just a talking point; it's a very real source of pressure that translates into statistics that might surprise you.

One in three teenage boys will engage in unhealthy weight control behaviors (it's one in two for girls), though many of the boys are actually trying to *gain* weight rather than lose it. It's this desire for bulk in the form of muscle that can drive them to take unstudied muscle-enhancing supplements or even known-to-be-dangerous anabolic steroids. Much more on that in a moment.

As for full-blown eating disorders, those happen for guys as well, more often than many people realize. When I was in medical school I was taught that 10% of anorexia cases occurred among males. Still to this day, 10% is the common-knowledge number thrown around everywhere from medical circles to parenting journals. So I was surprised to learn recently that the real number is actually much higher. Turns out, a full 25% of young people with anorexia are male. In fact, one-third of all people diagnosed with eating disorders of any type—not just health-endangering restrictive eating but purging and binge/purging, too—are male. This means that over their lifetime, between 2.5 to 3% of all guys will have a full-on, needs-treatment, parents-and-doctors-should-worry, we-thought-this-only-happens-to-females eating disorder. And to make matters worse, the risk of dying from one of these eating disorders is higher for guys because it is so often missed: most parents, doctors, teachers, and trusted adults aren't looking for the problem because stereotypically it isn't supposed to happen to boys.

There's a subgroup within the male eating-disorder subgroup that deserves special attention, and that's athletes who are essentially required to lose weight for their sport. This occurs particularly when a sport has weight classes (think wrestling, rowing, and horse racing) or an aesthetic component (gymnastics, swimming, diving, dance, skating, and—down the road, because this isn't exactly a big high school sport—bodybuilding). Studies show that across the board, about a third of all boys participating in one of these sports will struggle with body image issues to the point of developing an eating disorder. Now, by comparison, females face twice the risk. But unless you have a son who has struggled with this scenario, I bet you haven't thought about the extent of the issue among these particular boy athletes, because I hadn't and I am deep in this stuff all day, every day.

For the less serious but still-worrisome cases, meaning the folks who aren't labeled "eating disordered" but who do things like fast for weight loss or engage in extreme exercise, half are guys. Yes, half. But these issues, too, are generally labeled "female," and for precisely this reason males are less likely to seek treatment. It's not that they don't recognize the problem—many boys do—but rather that they feel an extra layer of shame about struggling with a "girl" issue, which often means they don't ask for help until it's too late, if at all.

The adults around eating-disordered boys tend to live in the dark, completely missing the symptoms and instead seeing them as "getting healthy." We adults often make the mega mistake of assuming our boys' lifestyles and physique changes mean they are on a path to more body confidence, not less. All the while and true to pubescent form, our boys stay quiet, increasing the likelihood we will overlook their extreme behavior.

HOW MASCULINITY DRIVES BOY BODY IMAGE

Masculinity is part psychology, part physique. On the emotional side of the equation, being masculine generally means guarding feelings, a convenient definition in light of the fact that boys generally get quiet when they enter puberty and begin their transformation into men who are expected to hold in worry, sadness, and vulnerability. That said, it's also classically manly to feel rage and show it; to be confident; and to take command. And these days, men are praised for expressing their vulnerability, stress, heartache, and confusion too . . . that is, as long as they still retain some element of being big and strong and macho. Emotional masculinity is kind of all over the map.

In contrast, the physical form of masculinity is quite specific and basically boils down to one word: *muscular.** The Abercrombie models, with their ripped abs and chiseled arms, represented the most masculine of barely adult males. This trope is nothing new—paintings and sculpture from ancient Egypt and Rome and China (to name a few far-flung antiquated spots) depict

---

* Okay, I just have to go down a semantic side path for a moment. How fascinating is it that if you look at the first six letters of "masculine" and the same first six letters of "muscular," they are almost the same? Now, I am no etymologist, but at least on cursory review, these words do not derive from the same root. Our use of them has made it seem as if they should, though . . .

torsos strikingly similar to the ones once walking around Aber-crombie storefronts but now relegated only to images on the bag. There had to have been in-the-flesh models for these art-ists to copy, each with a body screaming: *I can hunt for food! I can slay on the battlefield! I am a heavenly creature! I can bench-press more than my own body weight!* Whatever metric of social success was needed through the ages, this lean-but-not-too-lean, sculpted frame met it.

Which is all to say, there is a rationale for the ideal, muscu-lar, masculine body type. It's just not entirely rational, at least not anymore.

Lean is good, don't get me wrong. As is muscle mass. But when does the goal become problematic? We know for a fact that lower body fat and higher lean muscle mass predict better overall health, at least to a point. But do ripped biceps?

This is where the masculine ideal and the healthy ideal di-verge. A doctor-endorsed healthy body is radically different from a Calvin Klein underwear ad–worthy one, a distinction not always obvious to boys. When health care providers talk about *ideal body weight,* they are looking for a person to fall within a weight range determined by his height. The ratio, called Body Mass Index (BMI), predicts better overall health or at least less disease. That's why when we go to the doctor for a checkup, and when we take our kids in as well, we all stand on a scale and then place our backs to the wall or up against a measuring stick. From there is calculated our BMI: our weight (in kilograms) divided by our height (in meters) squared. No one in that office is looking at our abs or glutes.

Lots of people take issue with BMI as the benchmark for doctor-approved healthiness, precisely because it only reflects weight and height but doesn't account for muscle mass, body fat content, or cardiovascular health. This means that a per-son can be numerically on-target but still quite unhealthy. (Ever heard of skinny fat? It's a real thing.) Still, BMI is as decent a measure as the medical community has right now, and for most people, living inside an ideal BMI range is better than not.

Meanwhile, the social definition of "ideal," the one our sons learn first and foremost in the form of the perfect hero à la Superman and his friends and contemporaries, has nothing to do with a mathematical formula or even, frankly, weight. This cultural notion depends entirely upon appearances.

The pressure boys feel to look muscular is ubiquitous. It comes through all the channels we'd expect, like TV, film, ads, and celebrity influence, but also through one we might not: friends. In fact, more than two out of every three boys say it's their peer group that drives them to want to look a certain way. Some of this comes in the form of in-person ribbing, but social media delivers a hefty dose of peer pressure too. There are sites that peddle perfection (like Instagram), but also ones that allow kids to hurl questions out into the ether and wait for the volley of anonymous replies (if you haven't heard about Ask.fm or Sarahah, then dog-ear this page and go look them up). Friends' opinions—and I use the word "friends" loosely here—represent the biggest influence on boy body image, oftentimes parsed out in ways none of us parents ever could have imagined back when we were deep in puberty. While girls certainly sway one another's body ideals, they have also learned to rally around each other, supporting their friends who are struggling in this regard. Boys report the opposite: they feel the pressure, but none of the love.*

* According to Credos, a U.K. think tank funded by advertisers, media owners, and agencies, 23% of all young males believe there is one ideal body type. As part of a 2016 campaign called Picture of Health, Credos asked boys ages eight to eighteen if they were aware of digitally enhanced imagery and whether this impacted their attitudes and behaviors. They found that friends were the number one source of pressure and influence on looks. But they also discovered that while boys are more likely to talk to their friends about both looks and their feelings around their body than anyone else, they are also more likely to laugh off any issues for fear of social retribution like mockery and bullying. By comparison, girls tend to talk it out when friends make comments.

Doesn't matter if it's a billboard, a film star, or his best friend from eighth grade—and often it's all three—once a guy recognizes the value placed on the perfect male body, he may very well try to do something about it.

GETTING THE MUSCLES THEY WANT

When researchers drill down, about one-fifth of boys report being "highly concerned" about either their weight or their shape. Half of them want more muscles; a third want to be thinner *and* more muscular. But unlike girls their age, solely being thin is rarely the goal—frankly, it's often a worry. According to some studies, as many as 25% of normal-weight guys think they are too skinny, and up to 90% of all guys exercise with the goal of beefing up. This is the main reason why many parents are clueless about their sons' struggles with body image: our culture has really defined this issue through the female lens and therefore made it about weight loss, so it's easy to miss when boys are trying to gain weight and get fit.

How do they do it? The most common route taken by at least a third of all boys at some point during puberty (as reported in published data, though I personally think it's a gross underestimation) is to consume protein powders or protein-enhanced foods and drinks. It is worth educating ourselves about the actual healthfulness of these various products, because there's a huge range. Depending upon how processed they are, how much sugar is added, what else is thrown in there (like thickeners, vitamins and minerals, artificial flavors, or even straight-up chocolate), and the dose of protein consumed each day, these options can be unbelievably healthy or downright bad for you. But because of sensationalized labeling, it can be quite hard to tell the good from the bad. And did I mention that there exist no long-term studies of the effects of protein-supplemented diets in kids? So my general advice here for growing kids, and for fully grown adults as well, is to eat protein in the form of whole foods when available. Or, at the very least, consume proteins that cannot survive on a grocery shelf for three or four years. Our bodies are designed to absorb nutrients that grow in or on the earth, which explains why I am not a protein powder or bar fan.

Apart from the protein seekers, a smaller group—somewhere on the order of 10% of tween and teen boys—will use muscle-enhancing pills to grow their pecs and biceps. These come in two forms: either as a vitamin/supplement or a full-fledged medication. Let's start with the meds. Prescription drugs should be hard to get unless you need them for a legitimate reason—that's why pediatricians don't generally hand out prescriptions for medications like Epogen and growth hormone* when a kid is looking to build bulk. And so boys who seek muscle-enhancing meds must score them from people outside of the health care system, like teammates, school pals, and an ever-growing assortment of on-line sites delivering drugs to your front door. As a result, they may have no idea precisely what they are putting into their bodies. These aren't prescriptions dosed for them, nor are they coming from aboveboard pharmacists. You can see why taking prescription drugs to bulk up is bad for a growing kid on multiple levels.

Taking an over-the-counter vitamin or supplement isn't much better. Yes, these are purchased in a store, which feels far more legitimate than getting them from a friend or a coach or the Internet. But because they are supplements, by definition neither the store that sells them nor the manufacturer who makes them is required to check what's actually inside the bottle. The label can list almost any promise imaginable. It can attest to ingredients that go missing, miss ingredients that show

---

* So when would pediatricians prescribe these meds? Epogen is a blood builder. Kids with cancer often receive this drug, because chemotherapy can cause their blood cell levels to plummet; kids with anemia from chronic kidney disease or certain infections might get it too. Growth hormone is given to kids with short stature, growth hormone deficiency, or any number of syndromes associated with slow vertical growth, in order to help them attain height.

up, and claim doses wildly off the mark. Oh, and neither vitamins nor supplements face any requirement for safety testing either! Short of a consumer protection group calling for testing of a specific product, our boys are simply buying powders and pills because their promises seem trustworthy. It doesn't help that these bottles sit on the shelf at the local store right next to the (more legit) shampoo, foot fungus creams, and Tylenol. Why shouldn't their promises be trusted? By the way, the same warning about the safety and validity of supplements goes for everything we all purchase in this category. So think about that the next time you pick up a bottle of fish oil or vitamin D for yourself, and choose a brand that opts into testing.

The boys who are willing to risk the most in exchange for muscularity go beyond consuming extra protein or scavenging the local Walgreens for a muscle enhancer. These guys take *anabolic steroids*, a pharmaceutical-grade black-market drug. Anabolic steroids are the most well-known of the bodybuilding supplements, but also the ones used least often because you'd almost have to be living under a rock not to have heard of their risks. Unfortunately, some tweens and teens seem to live under rocks or choose to bury their heads in the proverbial sand nearby.

The unbelievably dramatic and dangerous side effects of anabolic steroids include: depression, rage (as in the famous 'roid rage), suicidal thoughts, and heart issues like cardiomyopathy. I have seen steroid users with all of these issues. I have also seen guys whose testicles shrivel up and penises shrink down, because anabolic steroids can do that, too. When I am teaching boys, I point this out first and foremost—they usually don't need to hear much more to dissuade them. I also remind them, and so I'll remind you too, that anabolic steroids are quite different from the steroids that a person might take for an asthma attack or an inflammatory disease. These latter steroids are *glucocorticosteroids*, and while they can interfere with sleep or make a person jittery, they don't shrink the family jewels. The good news is, only about 5% or 6% of guys will take anabolic steroids, which is not a small number—that's one in every class of twenty kids, spread over those kids' lifetime—but it's a lot fewer than the number drinking protein shakes or popping creatine and whey supplements.

One of the most impressive statistics of all is a summary stat: the vast majority of guys are willing to do something—some will do anything—to achieve muscularity. Studies show that as many as 70% of boys between sixteen and eighteen will buy a new product after seeing an ad, and a quarter will change up their exercise routine in the name of fitness. Ten percent say they would consider taking steroids to get there (consider, but not actually do it, which is a big difference but still . . .), while 12% would consider cosmetic surgery (again with that key word "consider"). These are staggering numbers, particularly high because boys were asked what they *might* do, not what they have done. But the pressure they feel is probably magnified by the fact that it's coming not just from the larger world around them but also from their close friends.

THE DOUBLE-EDGED SWORD:
FEAR OF FAT IN A WORLD OF OBESITY

It's a tricky dance to navigate conversations about overly enthusiastic fitness goals with some, and the need for healthy weight loss with others. Sometimes kids grapple with both simultaneously. We cannot ignore the reality that a third of American kids struggle with being overweight precisely when images of body goals flood their consciousness. And by the time our kids grow up to be middle-aged, despite the ideals and imagery around them, twice as many (that's two-thirds of all American adults) will carry too many extra pounds.

In the United States, almost 40% of today's adults tip the

scales so far that they qualify as obese.* Worldwide, the numbers are quite a bit less dramatic, but still . . . 13%. Obesity is an issue that ramps up over time, beginning for some in preschool, more in grade school, and by high school graduation it affects one out of every five kids. Factor in folks who are overweight but not technically obese, and we have just described 70% of the U.S. population over age twenty and 42% of the entire globe.

Being too heavy is unhealthy—no one doubts that. And yet pointing it out can be considered cruel. Most parents tell me their biggest fear is that, in an effort to help their kid get healthy and lose weight, they will set in motion a spiral toward issues around food or body confidence. Many parents of girls stay quiet because they worry about unleashing eating disorders if they say something to their daughters; many parents of boys remain silent because it's their dynamic with their son, and they just quietly hope he will grow into his heft.

There's no predictable path through growth, though, so the point at which a guy starts to sprout up varies widely. Some gain weight before stretching out—these boys might look heavier than usual for a few months before they gain an inch or more in height and redistribute the weight. Others stretch before gaining, which can make them appear especially string bean–ish at times. The boys who begin puberty carrying extra pounds may

---

* The definition of obesity is different for kids and adults. In the adult population, a BMI of 30 or higher qualifies (to be overweight, your BMI must be 25–29.9). Among kids, though, obesity is defined as a BMI greater than the 95th percentile. Now, this can be confusing, because the 95th percentile sounds like 95% of all kids weigh less. But not so. Instead, these percentiles are based upon graphs of often idealized populations. So when you read further down in the text that 20% of all high school graduates (or kids the age of high school graduates, because you don't need to graduate to be counted in this number) in the United States are obese, what that means is that 20% of all of these older teens weigh more than the 95th percentile, where we might logically expect 5% of the kids to fall. The numbers are complicated, to say the least.

slim down through the process, losing their "baby fat," but many tell me they don't trust their new proportions and fear the return of full cheeks and a belly. Still others gain and grow simultaneously, sometimes in desirable proportions but oftentimes not. And others continue to pack on pounds disproportionate to their height gain. No matter how their bodies morph, most boys feel self-conscious about the transformation, even wishing it could happen in a different way. (If that sounds familiar, it's because every book ever written about *girl* puberty covers this ground.)

We need to remember that boys are impacted by beauty standards too: they have a clear sense of what the perfect male body looks like, and two out of every three think it's attainable with enough effort. But it's not always achievable, nor is it necessarily healthy, especially in the most exaggerated form and depending upon how it was achieved. All of this leaves many boys traveling through puberty feeling inadequate, regardless of whether they are big or small, heavy or slim.

Yes, girls struggle with body image ideals, some tremendously and at great physical and emotional cost. But as a group, they get that female ideals don't sync with reality . . . Not so much our boys. Why? Because we don't talk about the male side of the equation, at least not often during adolescence. This isn't an at-fault situation, it's just where we have found ourselves as a culture, relegating talk about body pressure to the girls.

Here is where this dichotomy of conversation has landed us: more than half of all boys say they would struggle to talk to a teacher about an issue related to body image, and nearly a third couldn't—and wouldn't—talk to a parent. Meanwhile, the vast majority think that the perfect muscular male body is totally realistic and attainable, and when they begin to recognize how difficult it is to look like the Abercrombie guy, many are willing to do something unhealthy to get there. We adults need to start to see this. It is outdated to think that these are female struggles—they aren't.

Despite male pubescent quiet, we need to open up these specific lines of communication. Let's ask our sons what they think of the ideal body types plastered across billboards and screens. Let's talk about weight, stereotypes, diet strategies, and all of the rest of it before the world has that conversation with them. The longer we continue to overlook the forces that weigh on our boys, the more they have to manage on their own. In the context of not talking as much to our sons as we do to our daughters, the silence can be deafening, not to mention dangerous.

HOW TO TALK TO BOYS ABOUT . . . BODY IMAGE

Given the growing gap between healthy bodies and average ones, most of us have to figure out how to parent—or at the very least approach this third-rail topic—differently, especially in the years of maximal body transformation. Not all of these strategies will work for every family, but there's something for everyone on this list:

1. THROW AWAY THE SCALE. Not a talking strategy, but top of the list for a reason: kids don't need to weigh themselves regularly. If they feel the need, often there is something else going on.

2. SUBSTITUTE THE WORD "HEALTH" FOR THE WORD "WEIGHT." Weight is a yardstick that we have used to gauge health, but in a vacuum it means very little. If I weigh the same amount as someone who is a foot taller than I am, then either one of us is very heavy or one of us is way too light. Even when we talk about

weight for a given height, we are often focusing on the wrong thing.

3. BEWARE THE PROTEIN POWDERS AND BARS. Every pediatrician I know, myself included, recommends a healthy diet packed with whole foods and as light on the processed stuff as possible. This advice is born out of research that shows, unequivocally, this is the best way to feed ourselves. So, I just can't wrap my brain around recommending that kids—or anyone, for that matter, unless it's medically necessary—consume the least straight-from-the-earth form of protein imaginable. Want more protein? Eat it during meals with a knife and fork or spoon.

4. THAT GOES DOUBLE FOR THE SUPPLEMENTS. If you think a pill or drink that promises to help you bulk up in just the right places is too good to be true, you are right. Our bodies are designed to absorb nutrients through food—when we swallow those supplements in pill form, often the best-case scenario is that they go straight through; worst case, they don't . . . especially when you are taking something other than what you think you bought. Teach your son that unless he's got a specific medical issue and is being guided by a knowledgeable health care provider, skip the vitamin and supplement aisle altogether. And all of the miracle cures being peddled to him online, too. It will save him a ton of money, and possibly a medical fiasco.

5. MAKE BODY IMAGE GENDER-NEUTRAL. We have to retrain ourselves a bit here. Even if you are a parent who has talked to your son about body image (go you!), pay attention to how you do it. Call out boy-specific pressures, and feel free to compare and contrast with girl issues as well. If you have daughters, flip the equation for them from time to time, so that they can become sensitive to the boy piece here.

6. ASK FOR HELP. Body image is a massive topic. If you aren't sure that there's a problem—or if you just want to avoid one down the road—ask for help from the right resources. Start with your son's pediatrician, because that's the person who will be able to tell you whether weight is an issue for your kid. A good pediatrician can also have deep one-on-one conversations with your son to assess things like confidence and self-image. School counselors are also wonderful resources on this front. And remember to check in with your son's go-to person if you are worried: call his best friend's parent or his favorite family member if you need a little insight.

Chapter Nine
BOYS AND ADDICTION:
THE REWARD CIRCUIT STIMULANTS

ARE WE ALL ADDICTED TO SOMETHING?

I need my coffee in the morning. Cradling it between my cupped hands, even before the first sip (but definitely after), I instantly feel more alert and focused; without it, a dull headache emerges over the course of the first hours of the day. Just as profoundly—maybe more so—I *need* my phone. As I walk out of the house, the last thing I do is search, sometimes furiously, for the flat rectangle that can disappear deep inside my purse or into some mysterious corner of the house, and without which I feel disconnected from the world. Panicked, almost. It's absurd. But an addiction?

My son begs to play *Fortnite* and I allow it, to a degree. He has friends who seem to play at all hours, including while they ride in my car in a carpool situation, en route home to the bigger screen on which they will continue to play. And if these kids are not engaged in a game, they are often watching other players: the amateur and professional gamers who stream their battles, a completely bizarre phenomenon to me but not to any of the ten- or even twenty-year-olds I have ever asked. My son wouldn't say he "needs" *Fortnite*. He does, though, completely lose track of time when he plays, and more often than not he resists turning it off until I snap at him. He denies having a problem but, he tells me, he knows kids who are addicted.

Speaking of Snap, my daughter can have trouble staying focused on a conversation happening in real life if her phone is within arm's reach, because social media notifications beckon her. My endless suggestions to turn off notifications fall on deaf ears. But she's so aware of her phone's power that she often asks me to hold it while we are out somewhere, recognizing that if it's off her person it won't suck her in, but also acknowledging she feels naked without it in her vicinity, much like her mother. She says she doesn't want to become addicted.

There are the people who crave alcohol or marijuana or opiates; for others it's food or shopping or gambling—some are addicts, some are not. These days, I walk down the street ducking out of the path of gigantic plumes of vapor, evidence of the aerosolized nicotine the person in front of me just sucked into his lungs, and I wonder how he would categorize his desire for a drag. Is it a craving? A habit? Or does he have a need that must be met, an urge beyond his control, an addiction?

Many of us toss around the word "addiction" casually, because ingesting or applying or doing or playing—sometimes it feels like it could be almost anything—might trigger a *ding! ding! ding!* in our brain's reward center, and that chemical rush sets us up to figure out a way to have another. But there's a big difference between using the word addiction to mean craving or desire and addiction the disease. It's not that the former isn't an issue, but the latter can have devastating physical, emotional, and social ramifications.

Every parent wants to spare his or her kids a future grappling with these demons. But in a world where almost everything can be described (rightly or wrongly) as addictive, and where helicopter parenting is criticized for disabling our kids rather than helping them—generally a very fair criticism, by the way—how do we know when to run interference? Yes, there are hundreds of potential addictions, but most people will not become slaves to any of them. So, should you let your kid go to the party? Download a certain game on his phone? Hang out with a friend who makes the hairs stand up on the back of your neck? Take a sip of your drink? Have access to your credit card? Every family will arrive at slightly different answers, but effective parenting requires some form of limit-setting, at least until self-regulation kicks in. This chapter explains when you need to worry and why education, constraint, and delay might just be the trifecta of addiction prevention. (Plus help on how to talk about all of this with your kid, of course.)

WHY SOME PEOPLE BECOME ADDICTS

My first job out of college, I worked in an adolescent inpatient drug rehab center in New York City. I followed that gig with medical school and residency training in hospitals filled with drug-seekers, and then years in a pediatric office caring for families, among them new users flirting with or already committed to addiction. So I have known people managing these demons for the majority of my life. Generally good people; kind people; people across the age spectrum who weren't looking to get hooked—but then they did.

What they all had in common was a disease of feedback loops in the brain. Addicts engage in behaviors that turn on built-in reward centers, flooding the brain with overwhelmingly good (or, at the very least, less bad) sensations. As a society, we have become quite expert at recognizing addiction to substances, because it's pretty easy to draw a straight line between drinking or smoking or pill-popping and their range of physiological consequences: bloodshot eyes; slurred speech; stumbling gait; fantastical, irrational, or dumbed-down thoughts. We notice these because intoxication doesn't just signal danger to the person who is drunk or high, but it can put others in jeopardy as well—

that's why *don't drink and drive* has evolved from a warning to a slogan that transcends generations. And above all, we know what addicts will do to get their next high, which boils down to a willingness to prioritize the substance of abuse over the sanctity of the people around them.

Addiction in the drug and alcohol sense of the word occurs thanks to direct brain effects of pretty much any intoxicant, natural or man-made, prescribed, purchased, or scored. But an addict doesn't need to *take* something to feel a brain rush. The same neural circuits can fire when stimulated by things like intense exercise, gambling, gaming, shopping, even just scrolling on your phone and staring at your screen. So all of these things can be addicting too. The list of potential culprits runs long.

Every single addiction has a normal, non-addictive counterpart: lots of people drink in moderation, for instance, or exercise to a degree that's beneficial. We all shop and eat. In fact, far more people find a healthy balance with any and all of these behaviors than an unhealthy one. But moderation is elusive for the addict, who will often do or say almost anything in order to satisfy a craving, typically regardless of the consequences. The classic example from my days working in drug rehab: the addict who stole money from a parent's wallet, or even a TV off the wall, in order to fund his habit. It wasn't as if the missing cash (or TV!) would go unnoticed, but he didn't really care. At least not as much as he cared about feeling the chemical rush, the relief, the *ding!* in his brain.

Because that's what addiction is at its core: the pursuit of reward or relief, sometimes overt but often hidden under a veil of sneakiness and shame, making some addictions incredibly hard to spot. Porn addiction can go unrecognized outside of intimate settings, and shopping addiction can fly under the radar without credit card bills. Some addictions are more obvious since the consequences can be so profound. Drug addicts can overdose. Sex addicts can wind up with sexually transmitted diseases. Food addicts can develop obesity and a slew of related complications, from diabetes to cardiovascular disease. Addicted gamers have been known not to leave the couch even when nature calls. Yeah, it's pretty gross. Once recognized, the pathologies of addiction tend not to be subtle, which is why we can all conjure examples of friends or family members or even ourselves engaging in inimical behaviors in order to feed these brain reward circuits, despite negative consequences.

Why, then, do some people become addicted to certain substances or behaviors while most do not? The answer lies inside the brain, where whiffs of teeny-tiny chemical messengers called *neurotransmitters* leap from the end of one neuron to the beginning of the next, passing through the space in between called the *synapse.** There are several different types of neurotransmitters in the brain, and chances are you've heard of at least some of them—epinephrine, dopamine, GABA, and serotonin are among the most well-known. While the locations and impacts of each of these neurotransmitters is quite specific, really they just do one of two things: when released into the synapse, they either turn an electrical impulse on (that's called *excitatory*) or turn it off (*inhibitory*).

Dopamine is probably the most famous neurotransmitter at the moment, especially in the context of addiction, because it is the feel-good chemical: when it is released in certain parts of the brain (particularly an area called the *nucleus accumbens*), do-

---

*   The brain is a packed collection of roughly 100 billion nerve cells called *neurons*. Chapter 5 covers how the brain works—specifically how messages are sent, ideas conjured, and behaviors instigated—in great detail, but here's one piece that isn't discussed there. Neurons send signals among themselves and, eventually, out into the body using two different strategies: electric impulses travel down the long arm of a neuron and then chemicals (aka neurotransmitters) are released into the space (aka synapse) between the end of one and the beginning of the next. Once the neurotransmitters are received on the opposite side of the synapse, a new electrical impulse is triggered in the neighboring neuron. While it may seem inefficient for nerves to switch back and forth between two types of signaling, it turns out the electrical-plus-neurochemical system allows for extremely rapid messaging.

pamine is associated with elevated mood, motivation, and pleasure. It's also the common denominator in almost all addiction
scenarios. Depending upon the source—the drug or behavior,
that is—a different combination of neurotransmitters will be involved in the brain's response. So alcohol tells neurons to release
one combination of neurotransmitters, marijuana another, opiates yet another, and stimulants their own bespoke combo too.
Each of these drugs turns on unique concoctions of neurochem-
icals in specific areas of the brain, but dopamine always seems to
show up no matter what the impetus for the mental party.*

So, again, why do some people become addicts? Essentially,
because certain combinations of neurotransmitters in the synapses of specific parts of the brain feel good. *Really good*. And it
is human nature to seek replication of that feeling. The reward
circuitry of the brain was designed to make us feel great—or at
least super alert and highly sensitized—in certain settings. It
was also designed to be satiated and to weigh risks versus benefits. But addicted brains don't do this math in the same way.
When our ancestors figured out how to create a brain high
without some organic trigger (chased by a lion! having sex!) but
instead with intoxicants that allowed us to eat, drink, smoke, or
game our way to that feeling, our species was set up for addiction. Some brains comply more readily just by their very design.

Which begs the question of the genetics of addiction, because most people are curious or concerned about the family
tree factor. When trying to guess the likelihood that someone

---

* Drugs and alcohol each trigger increased dopamine in the reward circuits,
but in different ways. Some directly increase dopamine amounts, while others
change the environment of the synapse so that dopamine hangs out for longer.
The highs (and lows) of each of these pathways are different because each
substance of abuse involves other neurotransmitters as well. But the fact that
dopamine shows up at increased levels regardless of drug class is more than
interesting—it confirms dopamine's role in reward-seeking behavior, the common thread of addiction. And to strengthen that argument, dopamine appears
in the same common-denominator way in brains that are addicted to porn,
gaming, checking email while driving . . .

will become a drug addict, for instance, genetics account for about 50% of the equation, governing everything from the likelihood of starting to use to the chance that a person will develop dependence. So yes, if there's an uncle in rehab or a sibling who actively struggles with abuse, everyone in the biologically immediate family faces some increased risk. That said, exposure, resiliency, and culture also play critical roles. We call these outside influences *epigenetic variables:* factors in the environment that change the way genes express themselves. The list of epigenetic influences is so long it could occupy several pages— basically, anything that impacts anyone's DNA has epigenetic influence, from food to sleep to stress to love; from the chemicals that surround us to the steps we take to avoid them; from health (directly) to wealth (indirectly).

By design, the brain does have built-in checks and balances that protect most people from entering the cycle of addiction in the first place. But as you are about to see, they don't always work—especially when the brain isn't fully mature, and the check-and-balance system is not fully up and running.

LEARN THE SIGNS OF ADDICTION

These apply to drugs, alcohol, behaviors, even screens. All of our brains are vulnerable, even if we don't have a family history. So look for these signs in your kids and yourself. Even just one or two can be an early flag that there's a problem:

- Having trouble staying away from something that is negatively impacting quality of life.
- Experiencing a craving that is persistent, constant, or disruptive.
- Responding inappropriately or emotionally, with increased sensitivity, to stressors.

- With a given substance or behavior, the highs aren't so high anymore but the lows don't change (or they could get lower).
- Experiencing withdrawal—either physical symptoms or emotional despondence—when the substance or activity is not available.
- Willing to chase something despite negative consequences.

ADDICTION RISK IN A DEVELOPING BRAIN

The very fact that our kids' brains are still under construction makes them far more vulnerable to the addictive potential of everything from alcohol to drugs to porn to gaming.

This begins with the fact that their reward circuits are like soft clay, malleable and transformed by all of the forces they come into contact with. Our adult wiring, not nearly as much. Combined with the slow pace of myelination,* this explains why when a tween or teen finds himself in a situation where there's a primo opportunity to turn on his brain's reward circuits—this might be at a party where there's booze, or online where there's sex, or at school where there's access to a vaping device that allows a kid to take a hit of nicotine without the teacher noticing—the limbic system dominates decision-making. *Do what feels good,* whispers the devil over one shoulder, where the devil actually turns out to be rapid-firing electrical impulses reaching the limbic system in fractions of a second. The angel on the other shoulder hasn't

---

* Another quick Chapter 5 nod: remember that a fully functional check-and-balance system between frontal and limbic doesn't exist until they are both completely myelinated in early adulthood. Just like honing skills and expertise takes time, so does striking the ultimate equilibrium between going for it (limbic) and holding back (frontal).

even showed up because its impulses are still crawling along un-myelinated nerves toward the prefrontal cortex.

All of this is to say that the first reason why adolescents are more susceptible to addiction than adults is that their brains are still under construction, with the thrill-seeking centers dominating and then firing and then setting off intense positive feedback loops. The relative imbalance inside their heads means that tweens, teens, and even twentysomethings are slightly more likely to engage in behaviors with addictive risk rather than restrain themselves after weighing the long-term conse-quences. Humans of all ages will seek out things (foods, activi-ties, drugs, sex) to set our reward circuits afire, but younger humans with brains in the midst of being honed are especially teed up to find that stimulation. One key to becoming an addict rests in turning on the reward loop.

The second reason younger people are vulnerable to future addiction is that risk begets risk in a self-reinforcing way. At the very same time adolescents are engaging in feel-good behaviors with their reward circuits firing away, their brains are also prun-ing. Frankly, their brains are pruning when they are engaging in just about any behavior, so if they are studying math or learning to play drums, those skill sets get reinforced; and if they are get-ting high or playing video games, those skills are reinforced too. Remember from Chapter 5 the concept of "use it or lose it": neurons that fire together, wire together, while neurons that don't fire ultimately die away. Adolescence marks the time of maximal neuronal pruning and shaping—the kid learning a new instrument and loving it (fire, reward circuits, fire!) will pick it up faster than you or I ever could at our current age; the one learning how to get buzzed (again with the firing reward cir-cuits) will experience the same speedy learning curve.

It's the neurotransmitters in the synapses of the reward cen-ters of the brain—especially dopamine—that sit at the root of addiction. When kids get high or watch porn or game, a specific set of neurons fire, launching dopamine from their tips and essentially cementing themselves in the brain's hardwiring. Particularly when these behaviors are repeated over and over, there's little chance the brain is going to opt to kill off those heavily used neurons. Now, a "mature" brain is not entirely protective, because when adults engage in the same types of activities (and some number of adults certainly get high, watch porn, game . . .), they release dopamine in a very similar pattern. This is why adults can—and do—become addicts. But adolescents are more vulnerable than adults because their brains are not pre-pruned. Addicting substances and actions have the potential to become self-reinforcing in all brains, but especially in young, malleable ones.

Learning is the act of establishing neuronal pathways. As neurons fire in specific patterns, they hardwire themselves together. The first several times, creating these pathways takes effort. But with each subsequent firing, a pattern is established: a routine of electrical impulses followed by neurotransmitter release followed again by electrical impulse over and over along the same cells. Whether we are learning a computer program or a sport or a bad habit, the more often we tell our brains to fire a specific sequence of neurons, the easier it gets for our brains to comply, ultimately to the point of not even having to do any conscious work. Learning a skill and learning addiction are really not that different.

VAPING

E-cigarettes and other "smokeless" devices have actually been available for more than a decade, but in 2018 a new trend took hold among teens and tweens: Juuling.

Juul is a brand of electronic cigarette that delivers unbelievably high doses of nicotine to users. What made its popularity soar in the young population, a group, by the way, whose smoking rates were steadily declining until the emergence of Juul?

First, the device is sleek and sneaky. Its rechargeable battery looks just like a thumb drive, so kids can charge it in school without raising any suspicion. The delivery part of the device—the piece that contains vape-able liquid (called e-juice) and attaches to the battery—is long and slim, the perfect size to conceal in a closed fist or tuck into an athletic sock.

Second, the vapor generated from an inhale has no smoky smell, a feature shared by all smokeless devices.

Third, e-juice comes in flavors like Gummy Bear and Mango, flavors that very few adults might gravitate toward but lots of kids find appealing. In 2019, public health campaigns sought to prove that minors were being directly targeted as consumers, and eventually Juul pulled the sweet flavors from the market.

Fourth, Juul is marketed widely but beginning in 2018 the big push was through social media and influencers. In other words, where your kids are but you may not be.

And finally, an absurdly large number of kids believe that Juul e-juice is nicotine-free. It's not. In fact, one pod has the same amount of nicotine as a pack of cigarettes, and some studies show even higher doses. Nicotine, by the way, is highly addictive, ranking up there with heroin, cocaine, and amphetamines. Plus, e-juice contains bonus chemicals like propylene glycol and glycerol which combine to form the cancer-causing chemical formaldehyde.

Take all of these pieces and put them together, and you get a bonanza: a highly addictive drug until recently being marketed and delivered directly to kids and completely unbeknownst to us parents.

Part of the reason why Juuling caught on was precisely because parents remained in the dark. We don't smell smoke (although we can smell the air freshener–like scent of the flavors and wonder for a moment) and the device is easy to hide. This thing was so new that parents didn't even know to tell their kids not to do it, because they had never heard of it . . . until very recently.

Think your kid might be Juuling or using some other e-cig? Then start asking! Try not to be accusatory, because that often ends badly (not to mention with a denial). Instead share what you know and ask for information from him that fills in the gaps. Open up a dialogue about why and where kids vape. Asking questions about his friends tends to work better than going straight to asking about his own history, though it all depends upon how you and your son communicate in the first place. Most important, if he shuts down the conversation, keep going back and trying different approaches. The more often you ask, the more he will realize you care.

THE ADDICTIVE PERSONALITY?

When I was a practicing pediatrician seeing patients in the office all day, every day, one thing became very clear: some kids are born risk-takers and some simply aren't. Around nine to twelve months of age, as mobility really kicks in, there was a group of kids who would attempt to fling their bodies off my exam table with utter joy. Those were, by and large, the same kids whose parents would call me in a panic when at age two they were found scaling bookshelves, or at age five were zooming around on whatever wheels they could find (tricycle, bicycle, skateboard . . .) with as much speed as they could muster. They were often the ones to land in the emergency room for stitches, too. These kids were thrill-seekers to the core, and I often wondered if they were going to seek thrills in other ways as they grew older. Why wouldn't they? Risks felt good.

Now this doesn't mean that the babies who sat quietly, observantly, on the exam table, the ones who never tried to leap out of a crib and always proceeded with caution on trampolines or down slides at the park, were guaranteed to live safe, low-risk lives. They wound up in the ER with their fair share of stitches too! But any pediatrician will tell you that temperament is innately connected with behavior. When it comes to risk for addiction later on, I always worried just a little bit more about the babies who wanted to take a flier off my exam table.

Turns out, I wasn't so wrong. Studies have shown that there are temperamental traits associated with addiction—at least drug addiction—later in life. The traits fall into three general groups, but they all share the common theme of difficulty with self-regulation. One group of kids are impulsive, bold, and novelty-seeking. These are the ones that jumped out at me (often literally) at the office. Another group look quite the opposite because they are anxious or inhibited or even sad kids. Their risk for substance abuse is not thrill-seeking but rather self-medication, and most of them will explain that their early drug use didn't make them feel high and mighty, but rather normal. The last group of kids represent a combination of the first two, alternately daring and down, in and out.

Self-regulation is a learned skill, but it relies upon the brain being hardwired to be able to learn it. When a kid faces a consequence—be it a burn from touching a hot stove or suspension from cheating on a test—he learns to not repeat the mistake. In most cases, learning to self-regulate is etched into brain pathways beginning in infancy, so much so that older kids are able to compensate for the fact that their frontal lobes (home of long-term thinking) won't be mature for a few decades. Consider this: we teach our kids how to cross the street safely and then we trust them to stop, look both ways, and proceed with caution. They have self-regulated, resisting the temptation to run after a ball that's rolling down the street or a school bus driving away without them on it.

But in some brains, the underlying wiring isn't perfect, and even when kids try to practice the skill of self-control they lack the ability to master it. These kids (and adults) are impulsive, thrill-seeking, live-in-the-moment, YOLO types who are willing to try almost anything. Or they are so nervous and insecure that they simply cannot help themselves, and so they do the thing they know they shouldn't do or say the thing they know they shouldn't say. Some of these kids are withdrawn, compulsive, or even fearful; others are gifted or talented. Most of these kids, the fun-loving ones and the anxious ones too, are outliers, and it is their propensity to live in the extremes that puts them at elevated risk for addiction. They have what some people call an "addictive personality." So yes, addictive personalities exist—they don't, however, always appear the way we expect them to. And they are not a prerequisite to developing addiction.

Males and females are equally likely to fit into these personality silos. But it turns out that males are slightly less capable of self-regulation, broadly speaking. This means that they are a little more likely to engage in addictive behaviors . . . at least at first. It makes good sense that females evolved to have better self-regulation (really, it's better impulse control), because females have a limited supply of eggs—about four hundred total— that can one day become babies. Males, on the other hand, have a seemingly endless supply of sperm, churning out millions every day. If the ultimate goal for humans is to reproduce and make more humans, then males face fewer pressures when it comes to feeding, growing, and defending their offspring because they can make so many more genetic descendants. They don't need to delay their own gratification quite as much in order to pass along their DNA; they can prioritize self-control slightly less. In today's world, this translates into taking that drink or playing that video game or buying those shoes just a little bit more impulsively.

This is all to say that there's a reason why our girls are slightly less likely to engage in risk-taking behaviors than our boys. But once they do, and once those reward circuits begin firing regularly, females are just as likely to become addicts, and some studies show they are more likely to relapse after treatment.*

THE ANTIDOTE TO ADDICTION: DELAY

Our brains are designed to evolve and change with experience. This *plasticity*, as scientists love to call it, represents a blessing and a curse: brains that adapt quickly, learn rapidly. Young brains do this with enviable speed; mature adult brains more slowly. While addictive substances and behaviors can impact all brains, age definitely plays a role in how—and how quickly—they make their impact.

If a person really wants to reduce their addiction risk to basically zero, the only definitive way to do so is to stay away. From everything: drugs, porn, gambling, all of it. If you don't want your reward circuits to fire, don't give them reason to. This approach works, but it's not always compatible with life, particularly when we're talking about behaviors that we need to do in moderation (eat, shop), and those that if we do in moderation won't cause harm. It's also not very compatible with fun. This is why delay is often the parenting strategy of choice—teaching abstinence across the board doesn't work.

The secret to the success of delay is simple: if the young

---

* There's also science documenting decreasing impulsivity with increasing estrogen. As a result, and quite amazingly, females express more self-control during the phase of their menstrual cycle when they might get pregnant.

brain is more susceptible to addiction, then when it comes to just about anything that can land there, don't expose the brain until it has slowed down its learning curve. Let the brain fully myelinate, so that messages can zoom to all regions with equal speed, and thrill-seeking balances with rational thought. Give it time to prune neuronal pathways, reducing the likelihood of turning on reward circuits with something illicit or destructive. Time is our brain's best friend, at least insofar as making smarter decisions. Which is precisely why delaying experimentation with _____ (fill in the blank with absolutely anything that has destructive potential) is a winning strategy.

Delay is a prevention strategy that kids are often willing to embrace. We aren't saying *never*, we're just saying *not now*. As I've always told the parents of kids in my practice, starting when they are toddlers a kid's job is to push back, so we have to give them something to push back against. That becomes far more true in the tween and teen years. Knowing what we know about brain development and addiction, how can we not try to stave off risky experimentation when it could result in permanent hardwiring?

Laws subscribe to the philosophy of delay. Alcohol consumption is illegal until age twenty-one; recreational marijuana too, in the states that have deemed it legal in the first place. You can't rent a car until you are twenty-five unless you have a great driving record and you're willing to pay more (sometimes it's quite a bit more). But anyone can gamble by the time they are twenty-one, and some as young as eighteen in certain states. These laws and a slew of others like them did not derive from thin air—they relied upon data to show relative risk by age. Some align with the maturation of the brain (that would be you, rental cars, so well done!). Others seem to have tried to strike a balance between when the brain can best handle an exposure and the reality of the fact that kids are simply going to do it anyhow (that pretty much summarizes the drinking age). In a perfect world, our laws would coincide with our physiology, and that would help kids understand the limits. But it's not a perfect world, and every kid matures at a slightly different rate anyhow, so there isn't a right age limit that applies universally to any of this stuff.

Delay in a vacuum doesn't work nearly as well as substitution—there are only so many times we can say "No" without creating a whole other set of conflicts. But if our kids pivot their risk taking to safe outlets like sports, music, art, or even academics, the brain's reward circuits will still fire. It's that firing that feels so good. So while saying "No" can work, saying "No, but how about *this* thing instead?" tends to be a far better parenting strategy.

Here's the catch: as parents, we are much less likely to institute delay tactics for our boys if we don't know what they are doing, whom they are hanging around with, or how they feel—which is almost inevitable to some degree when they retreat and shut the door on us. Many boys are more subtle than that, choosing to share selective bits and pieces that we can weave together into a narrative of *Whew, he's all right*. But when they go quiet, or just quieter, an information gap emerges. Without knowledge of what they are doing, it's nearly impossible to try to convince them to slow down. When we accept that they live behind permanently shut doors, we have no idea what they are doing in there (vaping? gaming? getting high? bingeing?), let alone how it might morph into a future problem. When we lose track of their social networks, we relinquish the ability to help them identify good and bad peer influences. When we don't engage our boys in conversation, our parenting competes directly with a rapidly developing brain, where *dings!* in the reward circuitry result in powerfully positive feelings, the top of the slippery slope toward addiction. Sure, we can have broad-strokes conversations in advance—don't drink, vape, gamble, etc., etc.—and well we should! Prevention is a far better approach than treatment. But even prevention becomes tricky when our boys get quiet.

———

By the time our kids hit adolescence, most of them have mastered our buttons and vulnerabilities. They know how to rationalize, explain away, and even pull the wool over our eyes. I sit in awe of the few parents who are completely unshakable. Most of us give our kids the benefit of the doubt, choosing to see life as a series of growth experiences . . . that is, until they get themselves into trouble, and then we feel awful for missing the early signs.

Kids and adults alike are vulnerable to the same cycle of wanting to feel good—or at least to feel not bad. Having a fully mature brain is not a perfect safeguard against becoming an addict, but my brain and your brain can withstand stimulation that our sons' brains cannot. And when there's a phone or computer in that sealed-off room, we have no sense of what they are doing on the screen and how that activity is impacting their reward centers. Ditto when there's a vaping device, a credit card, or a fifth of liquor stashed in there. When we honor our boys' desire to go quiet rather than talk things through, we risk missing the details of what is happening within their social networks, or their bodies, or both. Each one of these hurdles makes it increasingly difficult to protect our sons from behaviors that can slip down a slope toward addiction.

HOW TO TALK TO BOYS ABOUT . . . ADDICTION

Addiction prevention can feel like an enormous undertaking, especially if we're talking about everything from alcohol and drugs to gaming, porn, and gambling. But the core tenets are the same regardless of the addiction you are trying to help prevent.

1. BE THE FALL GUY. Parents, don't expect your kids to have superhuman strength. Encourage them to make you the bad guy when other kids are offering them

something they don't want to try. Let them know that they can completely throw you under the bus with their friends—describe you as prudish or tough as nails or even slightly insane—if that helps them not to partake.

2. SAVE YOUR SON FROM SITUATIONS THAT MIGHT END BADLY. If you think that everyone is going to be drinking or getting high at the party, you don't have to let him go. If there's not going to be an adult nearby, but instead an older sibling is "chaperoning," alarm bells should be going off. It's A-OK to say: *No, you just can't.* If that's not an option because it's going to land you in the midst of World War Three, then scramble to make a family plan that he has to be a part of, like dinner with grandparents; or organize something that you know he'll be into, like getting tickets to a concert or a movie on opening weekend.

3. WHAT TO SAY IF YOU THINK THERE'S ALREADY A PROBLEM. This depends heavily upon the type of relationship you have with your son. If you can speak openly with each other, then start by saying something very straightforward, such as: *I am worried about you because* . . . Even if you have incredibly open family communication, avoid doing this in front of his siblings, because he shouldn't need to manage that shame along with your concern. If your communication is hit-or-miss, set up the conversation for maximal success. Generally, this means catching your son at a good moment, when you can have a calm back-and-forth, rather than leveling an accusation when he's already riled up about something else. Many parents want help with how to approach their kids, for which there are lots of outstanding resources. Start with your pediatrician or a school counselor whom you trust. If you have a relationship with a therapist, you can lean on that, too; if not, you might seek a referral to one.

4. WHAT ABOUT DRUG TESTING? I have been amazed by the number of kids who tell me they want to be drug tested. Why? Many say it's the excuse they need to get out of a peer pressure situation. Others say it's a means to stop themselves from giving in to an impulse. Whether kids actually want this looming out there or not, the most important piece of advice I can offer is this: never drug-test your kid without his knowledge. Because if he tests positive, you suddenly have a big problem if your son doesn't even know he was being checked in the first place. Trust is paramount to communication.

Chapter Ten
BOYS AND GUNS: AGGRESSION AND VIOLENCE, FROM SCHOOLS TO SCREENS

THE VERY FIRST SCHOOL MASSACRE ON American soil occurred in 1764 in Pennsylvania. A small group of Native Americans reportedly captured schoolmaster Enoch Brown and eleven of his students, killing most of them by clubbing and scalping. No firearms seem to have been involved, but this still goes down in history books as our first incident of mass killing at a school.

It was almost a hundred years until the next reported event—emphasis on "reported," because having none officially accounted for doesn't mean they didn't happen. Then, through the second half of the nineteenth century and the first half of the twentieth, accounts emerge of isolated school-based incidents, usually adult-on-adult violence triggered by grievances over employment issues or personal dramas. In 1940 at a school in South Pasadena, California, a recently fired junior high school principal shot and killed six school officials, the deadliest shooting incident at a school to that date. School shootings have continued in a steady stream ever since, with one major pivot: they began to feature students. The 1970s marked a particularly brutal period because not only was violence instigated by students, but there were also mass-casualty attacks against students at the hands of police (Jackson State University) and National Guard (Kent State University).

The stakes rose again in 1999 when two teenage boys massacred a dozen students and a teacher at Columbine High School in Littleton, Colorado, a rampage ending with the shooters' own suicides. As I type, the record for the school shooting resulting in the most devastating tally goes to Virginia Tech, where in 2007 a student killed thirty-two fellow students and faculty—I pray this sentence isn't outdated anytime soon, let alone before this book is published.

School shootings have become hideously commonplace in the U.S., so much so that my kids have active shooter drills more often than they have earthquake drills, and we live in California literally on the San Andreas Fault. This doesn't mean, though, that schools are the most common sites of homicides in this country—they're not, in the slightest. In fact, they only account for a tiny fraction of the 35,000 annual gun-related deaths in the United States. Even among youth homicides, each year only about 2% are school-based. But because we like to think that schools are—or should be—safe havens, many parents now feel the stir of a little pit of worry at drop-off each morning.

And then there's this: when scanning the list of the twenty-five deadliest school shootings—including Sandy Hook Elementary (2012; twenty-eight dead), Marjory Stoneman Douglas High School (2018; seventeen dead), and Umpqua Community College (2015; ten dead)—all of the perpetrators were male, and all but six were under the age of thirty.

The fact that the vast majority of school shooters in modern history have been tween, teen, and twentysomething males cannot result from coincidence alone. Far beyond schools, we have a much bigger, more systemic shooting problem in this country—a problem that keeps expanding, particularly among young males in the throes of, or not so far out the other end of, puberty. The age range of these boys overlaps precisely with imbalance in the developing brain, when the impulsive limbic system rules. How does biology interact with maleness in a society overflowing with accessible guns, violent video games, and rising cases of reported anxiety, depression, and psychological trauma? And how should we parent our sons in this deadly culture?

RELATIVE RISK: PUTTING SCHOOL SHOOTINGS INTO PERSPECTIVE

Even the term itself, *school shooting*, sends chills up the spine. These two words do not belong together, which largely explains why these mind-numbing events get so much coverage. But ever since Columbine, school shootings have become a routine American phenomenon, with an average of ten per year.[*] These episodes sit within a much larger context of guns and violence in general, so before drilling down on campus terror, it's important to understand the big picture.

The United States has a hideous record when it comes to death by gun violence. Worldwide, about a quarter of a million people die every year as a result of gunshots. Half of these deaths occur in one of six countries: Brazil, Mexico, Colombia, Venezuela, Guatemala, and the United States. If you are the type that likes keeping score, we hold the number two slot, just behind Brazil. Now, the United States has the biggest population among this group of countries, so when taking that into account our rate of firearm deaths (10.6 per 100,000 people)

---

[*] This is an incredibly tricky number to pinpoint, actually, because school shootings are accounted for in many different ways. When it comes to gun violence at schools, every database seems to record something different. Some account for any shooting that occurs on a school campus, whether or not there were injuries or deaths. Others will only list mass school shootings, events that, by definition, kill at least four people. In this chapter, I am relying upon the latter because databases tend to be more consistent here, which means that the average number of "events" will be on the low end. But suffice it to say that even one school shooting is tragic. That I am racking my brain trying to come up with an accurate average tally here is a sad, sad statement.

falls lower on the list—below the others in the top six and more impoverished nations that presumably lack the resources or the structure (or both) to handle social inequities. But our ranking still soars high above those of other wealthy nations: the gun death rate in the United States is nearly four times that of Switzerland (2.8 per 100,000), five times Canada (2.1), and thirty-five times the United Kingdom (0.3). These are all-population statistics, which means the numbers skew heavily toward adults. When we look specifically at kids, in the United States their chance of dying by gunshot is still 4 per 100,000, with boys representing more than 80% of that number. This last statistic means that American children are 36 times more likely to be killed by firearms than kids in other high-income countries, where the average rate of gun death is closer to 0.1 per 100,000.*

Gun ownership in the United States has remained fairly steady over the past four decades, with anywhere between 37% and 45% of all households reporting at least one firearm. That said, there are more guns in the world today than when we were growing up, and Americans own nearly half of the world's total supply. While about 50% of all American gun-owning households contain only one or two weapons, the other half have three or more, with a sizable subgroup (around 7.7 million "super-owners") owning an average of seventeen firearms. Still, despite the impression left by these daunting numbers and news coverage of firearm incidents, chances are that none of us will ever know a school shooter or be involved in a mass shooting. Statistically speaking we are far more likely to be impacted by accidental homicide, domestic gun violence, or suicide by firearm.

At least in America, death by gunshot is most commonly a

---

* Firearms are actually the second-leading cause of death among U.S. children, behind motor vehicle accidents. These two are often lumped together in the general category of "injury," sometimes making it hard to tease the numbers apart.

result of suicide. In other words, a person living here is more likely to use a gun to kill himself than someone else. This is an incredibly important point—and not true of most other places, by the way. The suicide piece of the equation makes the whole gun violence conversation trickier, because we really need to have at least two separate dialogues: one about what drives violence against others and one that asks why people seek to end their own lives. These threads are quite distinct, but they get consolidated when the focus is on the tactics (guns) rather than the root problem (who is being killed—others or self). It also bears mentioning that suicide by gun is far more male than female. When females want to harm themselves, they tend to opt for pills or suffocation, whereas males reach for firearms.

Accidental homicide represents another significant bucket of deaths caused by guns. Stories abound about these totally unintentional incidents—essentially nonviolent shootings, the ultimate mistake. They are the reason I role-played with my kids for years about what to do if they were ever over at a friend's house and suddenly found themselves in a situation involving a firearm. Working in the hospital and in my practice, I heard countless tales detailing the devastation that follows two kids playing around with a gun.

Our shooting problem has multiplied because of the simple math of gun availability: there are more guns than people in the United States. In 2017, the number of civilian-owned firearms in this country was 120.5 guns per 100 people. If these numbers perplex you, that's because they suggest that there are enough privately held guns in America for everyone to have one, and then some—the highest per capita rate in the world. In a distant second place, Yemen reported 52.8 civilian-owned firearms per 100 people, and Montenegro and Serbia tied for third with 39.1 per 100 people. Given the sheer number of weapons in circulation in the United States, it's no wonder we have a gun crisis both on school campuses and off.

A note on word choice, because this skews the statistics,

sometimes dramatically. A *school shooting* is a shooting that takes place on a school's premises or at a school-sanctioned function; a *mass shooting* is one where the shooter kills at least four others. Both are awful. But the distinction between them leads to very different data sets because school shootings aren't always mass shootings—in fact, most of the time they're not, with more than 90% of school shootings having one, two, or three victims.* The reverse is also true: mass shootings happen all over the place, not just schools.

Even though we've already had as many mass shootings in the first eighteen years of this century as during the prior sixty years, they aren't as common as headlines may lead us to believe: mass shootings account for a tiny percentage (many sources put it at less than 2%) of gun deaths in the United States. That said, gun violence is typically measured by the number of people killed, not injured. This means that an incident where a gunman opens fire at a large group and injures many but kills fewer than four is not counted as a mass shooting; if he injures many but kills none, it's not recorded as a shooting at all. Almost all of the deadly shootings in this country have only one or two fatalities, and beyond that there's really no central accounting for the number of people whose lives are forever changed by gun violence—from those paralyzed by spinal cord injuries to those paralyzed by fear.

This is all to say that while these days, when the words "shooting" and "kids" are uttered in the same breath, it's easy to assume that an indictment of mass violence on school campuses will follow. But the reality is that shootings occur all over the place, the vast majority not on school campuses. And kids are killed by guns for a whole host of reasons, not just because

---

* Most involve just one or two. It's interesting that the rate of these homicides hasn't budged in the past twenty years. Not so for multiple-victim mass shootings, though, which have risen steadily since 2009 and sharply since 2016.

violence and aggression have found their way into school cafeterias and English classrooms and locker-filled corridors. The issue of gun violence in this country is massive—I am only tackling one corner of it.

THE PROFILE OF A (SCHOOL) SHOOTER

Males dominate the gun story, on both the aggressor and victim sides, in schools and on city streets too. Nearly all mass shootings are committed by males; in fact, around 90% of all homicides in this country are at the hands of males and more than 80% of suicides by gun. Males own most of the guns in the United States as well, outnumbering female owners three to one. According to UCLA law professor Adam Winkler, a Second Amendment scholar and author of *Gunfight,* "Gun violence is often portrayed as a mental health problem, but it's not, it's actually a male problem."

I am going to focus on school shooters for a moment, because this chapter, let alone this book, isn't long enough to dive deep into the myriad reasons why some boys turn guns against themselves, others against rivals, and still others against complete strangers. I also believe that the typical profile of a school shooter explains a lot about what underlies gun violence within boy culture. That said, there isn't exactly an archetype here, despite our craving for one. Many people want to believe that school shooters are all withdrawn loners, trench coat–wearing social outcasts whose slumped posture and dark demeanor would have served as giveaways if only someone had been watching for them. Sure, this image fits some of the assailants, but it certainly doesn't describe them all. They can be charismatic and social, too. They cross every socioeconomic, racial, and ethnic line. Some come from fractured homes, but others were raised by two parents in a stable family, at least according to the shocked neighbor who always seems to score a TV interview. Some of the shooters carry mental illness diagnoses, but many do not; and even if they do, the types of mental illnesses often cited and on the rise don't beget aggression or violence, so they don't explain the upward school shooting trend: neither depression nor anxiety nor ADHD makes a person more likely to be homicidal. If only there was a single profile, it would be so much easier to identify early on the kids at risk for becoming threats to other kids. It's not that anyone wants to pigeonhole them, but rather save lives, the shooters' included. This has proved nearly impossible.

The overwhelming majority of modern school shooters do have four fairly predictable traits, though: they tend to be male, young, with access to weapons, and have a history of some sort of exposure to trauma. This tetrad of the typical school shooter turns out to be a list of qualities that often describe boys brandishing guns across the board, inside and outside of schools.

Maleness. Ninety-five percent of school shooters are guys.[*] We know testosterone is at play in some capacity, at least insofar as aggression and dominance are concerned, but there is so much more than this one hormone that piles on to the male experience of growing up. The element at the heart of this book is retreat: when boys enter puberty, not only does their internal chemistry shift, but they get quieter. As a result, when they struggle along the path to manhood—whether socially, academically, or even psychologically—their hardships can be missed. This is especially true in a culture that defines masculinity as physically tough and mentally stoic: we normalize boy quiet and don't always probe. Even when we do, we can easily overlook

---

[*] According to FBI archives, fewer than 4% of active shootings happen at the hands of females. But that said, one of the very first modern-day school shooters was a teenage girl named Brenda Spencer, who lived across the street from a California school. One morning in 1979, she shot at children from her home sniper-style, injuring some and killing the two adult males trying to usher the kids to safety.

the signs of deep humiliation or perceived failure, especially if a typical response from our sons is a grunt and a closed door. Some boys lack empathy—some girls, too—but the less we engage with our sons in regular day-to-day small talk and banter, the fewer clues we have to this pathology. All of this plays a role in the evolution of toxic masculinity: the emotionless, tough-guy persona that increases boys' likelihood of shifting from aggressive to aggressor.

Sue Klebold, the mother of one of the two Columbine shooters, gives an incredible TED Talk in which she describes parenting a child who turns out to be a cold-blooded killer. She never suspected a thing. She missed all possible signs because, at least through her lens, there were none: he seemed like a normal kid, managing his own hiccups and hurdles at school and within friendships, not talking to her as much as the next guy doesn't talk to his mom—nothing out of the ordinary. She only learned about his deep depression months after his own death. While he was alive, Sue Klebold's son's emerging quiet was expected for an adolescent boy, and his silence as deeply entwined with evolving manliness. It was not an unreasonable perspective, as I've pointed out several times. But it turns out that breaking this silence might have been the key to identifying him as an outlier, and then saving him from himself.

Youth. Most school shooters are teens and twentysomethings, either current students or recent ones returning to the primary site of their coming-of-age. Their brains have not yet fully matured, and so they lack the ability to make consistent rational long-term decisions the way an adult can (Chapter 5 has a lot more on this). That said, most shooters have planned their attacks—these are not impulsive acts but the result of weeks or months spent devising, stockpiling, organizing—so we cannot blame impulsive decisions due to unfinished hardwiring in the brain. Most school shooters don't "just snap."

Still, the risk/reward equation is different for adolescents and adults, as is problem-solving. Youth may contribute to a belief that weapons are a solution to a problem, particularly a social humiliation that in high school or college can feel like the end of the world but in hindsight, not. Add this to *neuroplasticity*, that feature of brain cells that reorganizes and maximizes their connectivity with use. Young brains, growing and pruning, are particularly influenced by the world around them; and as a result, exposure to violence begets violence. But by the time their brains reach adulthood, they have often learned other strategies. This is good news: because of neuronal flexibility, adolescent brains are capable of reversing course. Older brains can tap into nonviolent solutions, even when those same brains were steeped in violence years before.

Access. Two out of every five homes in the United States have guns, and among these, 55% have at least one stored in an unlocked location. In other words, kids often have easy access to the tools necessary for a shooting. Studies show clearly that living with a firearm dramatically increases the risk of both homicide and suicide. Three-quarters of all kids age nine and younger living in a home with a gun know where it's stored; one-third of them report handling the weapon, even when their parents think the gun is secretly hidden. The numbers for older kids are presumably higher. Beyond this, over the past several decades a trend has evolved toward armed teenagers leaving the house with their own weapons. This pattern escalated so dramatically in the early 1990s that metal detectors began to appear as a preventive measure at schools, aiming to identify not only intended shooters but also just kids packing heat.

It turns out that most firearms used by youths in school shootings came from their own home, a friend, or a relative. Ditto for firearms used in off-campus gun violence. Having the ability to obtain weapons is a basic prerequisite for becoming a shooter. The reverse is just as true: without access to a gun, it is impossible to shoot someone.

Trauma. Trauma is a humongous category. Almost any accident, natural disaster, assault, injustice, illness, injury, instability, source of stress or pain or loss falls into this basket. What human hasn't experienced some degree of trauma? Arguably, very few.

It's interesting, then, or maybe overwhelming, that having a history of trauma is a risk factor for becoming a perpetrator of violence. Turns out this is especially true when trauma is combined with mental health issues that reduce a person's ability to cope with stressors—conditions like severe depression or paranoia. One classic example is the experience of being an outcast: the kid who is rejected by his peers (that's the trauma) may have some underlying anxiety, depression, aggression, or antisocial traits (the mental health issues) that further drive others away from him. Most kids survive their traumas, and many thrive beyond them. However, the few who devolve into violence tend to follow a course that goes something like this: the trauma causes humiliation, which breeds anger and blame and then, ultimately, unless coping strategies are in place, a revenge fantasy. Along this entire path—and there are many different variations of this path—there are multiple points of potential intervention, but each requires that a kid is seen and heard. If there is no adult who recognizes what is happening, there is often no one to stand in the way of unfolding tragedy.

None of these descriptors—youth, maleness, access, or trauma—are sufficient. In fact, millions of people fit all four descriptors and will never reach for a weapon, let alone aim it at another human. And violent acts are committed by people who defy each of these categories. But among those who have engaged in gun violence, and especially within the tiny group of individuals who have terrorized kids on school campuses or at school events, the majority check all of these boxes. They are young, they are male, they have suffered some sort of trauma, and they can get their hands on a gun.

WHAT ABOUT VIOLENT VIDEO GAMES?

There's a lot of buzz about violent gaming—particularly first-person-shooter games—as an underlying motivator of gun violence. Study after study has failed to find a causal link, but before we jump on that data, let's pull the lens back. Because even without guns and ammo on the screen, there's clearly a psychological impact to the experience of almost any genre of video game play.

Gaming clearly impacts mood. This came up in my practice almost daily, and I definitely noticed it in my own home when my then young kids even played "educational" games. There would be times I tried to take a device away only to be surprised by their utter refusal to hand it over. But the first time I bore witness to the full-psyche impact of video games was when my son was about ten. This marked the start of begging and pleading to play something, anything, on a screen. *Super Mario Bros. FIFA. Candy Crush.* He didn't seem to care what kind of game or what medium he played on, from a palm-sized mobile device to a massive wall-mounted TV; he just wanted to engage. When we did let him play, we held tight to a pre-negotiated rule that forbade violent games, and he seemed fine with that.

But after about forty-five minutes, it was as if some sort of switch tripped in his brain and my charming little guy, who would do just about anything I asked in exchange for game time, became highly resistant to our efforts to get him to stop. Before forty-five minutes, we could tell him to finish playing and he might protest for a moment, but he'd still comply. After the magical three-quarters-of-an-hour mark, though, he devolved into a whiny, insistent, sometimes even argumentative version of himself. Gone were the niceties of polite requests to keep playing, replaced by demands that he must finish a particular game or level. This was with *benign* games, by the way, not an ounce of aggression tucked inside them; they still flipped some sort of switch inside his brain.

Every parent I have ever asked describes a similar phenomenon; when I speak to parent audiences on the topic, heads nod furiously in agreement. After some amount of gaming—for my son at that particular age, it was forty-five minutes—it can feel like our kids have been hijacked, replaced with moody, even oppositional versions of themselves. And while this temporary behavior shift has nothing *directly* to do with the fear of raising a child who will become gun-violent, it reminds me every single time I see it that gaming of any sort impacts the psyche, which in turn makes me wonder if the studies looking at the impact of gaming on violence are actually looking at the wrong things.

Our experience of battling against game turn-off was how my husband and I landed on an endpoint rule: No gaming beyond emotional impact, which for our son meant no gaming beyond forty-four minutes (I tell you, minute forty-five got ugly when he was younger).* It went without saying that there would definitely be no violent games.

And then came *Fortnite.*

This multiplayer, multiplatform shooter game, void of blood and guts, launched in the summer of 2017 and passed 200 million registered users within eighteen months, setting a new record for video game success (and a big fat new denominator for scientists to use in studying game effects). In the world of *Fortnite,* a player's avatar is visible in the foreground of the screen, which is what makes it third-person—in contrast, in a first-

---

* We weren't perfect timekeepers, so the rule was more like a goal. But the behavior shift was predictable enough that I became motivated to set an alarm on my phone. Otherwise, if I got busy doing something else and forgot about the fact that my son was gaming (who hasn't done that when their child is quietly, happily immersed in a device?!), I suffered the consequences of having a less-than-likable kid when the game was finally turned off. Interesting side note: As a big believer in explaining why a rule is set, I explained the rationale and my son agreed. Try asking your kid how they feel after gaming for prolonged periods of time. You might be surprised.

person-shooter game the images on the screen are viewed through the eyes of the player as the aggressor. This distinction is subtle, but critical to *Fortnite*'s success. It's also part of what makes *Fortnite* highly profitable, because that avatar can be dressed in costumes called "skins" or programmed to break out in victory dances, each for a small (cash) price. It's a fully sanitized version of a shoot-'em-up, showing no gore. And it's highly social, with team play encouraged thanks to the ability to connect experientially through the game, and verbally on headsets (sold separately, of course).

We had a rule about violent games—none—but as other parents rapidly embraced *Fortnite*'s brilliant PG approach, we began to question ourselves. No blood, guts, or sexism, and players even build things while trying to survive! Still, though, the goal was to trade up weaponry in order to outlive everyone else—a violent game that bizarrely doesn't look so violent. Everyone our son knew was suddenly part of this social phenomenon, and so we gave in. On the upside, there was no difference in his behavior while playing this game versus any other: as long as we kept to our time limit, he was happy to get off and frankly agreeable, at that. But if I let the prearranged amount of time pass by—if I forgot about the game that was on in the other room, because the house was quiet and I was getting life accomplished—when I eventually remembered, I didn't just face moodiness; I had to dodge a volley of complaints about "finishing the round" and cries of unfairness because "no one else has to get off" while simultaneously watching my son furiously snipe at other players in an effort to eradicate them. Despite a commitment to non-violence in our home, I realized we had become part of the rapid downward reach of gun-based gaming into middle (and even grammar) schools.

Here's my issue with shooting games. The data doesn't show what I see in my house and what I hear from so many others: that kids on games seem agitated after playing for a long enough time; that they act like they are traumatized, or at least jacked-up on endorphins. Combined with what looks a whole lot like desensitization to shooting and killing, how can there not be at least some link to real-life violence? Forget *Fortnite*, which seems downright child-friendly by comparison—how about first-person-shooter games filled with gruesome detail?

Despite my observations, though, according to multiple studies, the data actually show the opposite. They suggest *benefits* from first-person-shooter video games—big ones, like improved spatial skills, changes in neural processing and efficiency that boost attention, and even enhancement of creative thinking. And what's more, rates of overall youth violence have actually decreased as violent video game consumption has increased—not that this is necessarily causal, but it's important to point out. Herein lies the foundation for the biggest argument against violent gaming inspiring real-life shootings: these games are available and played worldwide, so if they spur violent behavior among players we should be seeing evidence of that everywhere these first-person-shooter games are embraced, which is pretty much across the globe. But we're not. So, yes, there are more graphic shoot-'em-up games to be purchased or downloaded—and played—than ever before, but many studies argue that this fact is neither increasing nor decreasing global gun violence, especially at schools.

Clearly, I really struggle with the vindication of violent video games. I don't refute their measured benefits; it's just that I cannot convince myself of their lack of harm. Maybe the reason that gamers in other countries don't take up arms of their own in real life is simply a function of lack of access to weapons. It's hard to land anywhere certain in a circular argument, but many of the developed countries where these games are popular also have far more stringent gun laws than the United States.

It seems to me that uber-violent games belong on the list of common features of shooters, alongside maleness, youth, access, and trauma. Actually, perhaps as a subtype of trauma. Maybe even the primary subtype. Because there's no denying that first-person-shooter games turn on the biological stress response—even third-person-shooter games do this, and I would argue G-rated games do to some extent as well. If you doubt me, just go watch people of all ages as they play; it almost doesn't matter if it's *Super Mario Bros* or *Mortal Kombat*: hunched over, intensely focused, eyes squinting, oftentimes snappy when you attempt to have a conversation with them while they are mid-round. But the violent games also normal-ize—or at least game-ify—brutality, which must on some level be traumatic. Right? So, despite the fact that there's no defini-tive evidence drawing a straight line between first-person-shooter video games and taking up arms, it feels like there is a clear case to be made for somehow connecting those dots . . . or at least a mandate to prove once and for all that they do not tie together.

If "use it or lose it" is the key to hardwiring future brain skills, then all of these shooting games, first- or third-person, carve paths in our kids' heads for sure, especially because gam-ing thrives on active participation, not passive viewing like a TV show or movie. Plus, they reward kills. Even more brain-stimulating, the character in both first- and third-person-shooter games is a version of you, an avatar that runs, ducks, snipes, and otherwise brutalizes through your lens. In third-person-shooter games, the avatar may not resemble you in the mirror, but there is still a clear emotional connection between the person holding the controller and the character whose POV is portrayed on screen. So the aggression played out and re-warded through these games is also rewarded in the brain. That, at least in my opinion, is the clearest downside to all of this: aggression turns on the brain's reward circuit, and so if there's a real-life opportunity to do the same, it feels at least plausible that one might engage. Thus the flurry of research trying to answer this very question.

In my house, before *Fortnite*, "No" sufficed. We didn't own gun-based games, and so even if my son played them at friends' houses (he later told me he did), his exposure was limited. But in a post-*Fortnite* world, where characters never spill a drop of blood—instead they only ever break out the dance moves, some of which are quite awesome—"No" morphed into a time-restricted and highly qualified "Okay." Meanwhile, I am left wondering things like: How should we categorize this scrubbed-down form of violence? And what's the impact of aiming to be the sole survivor on an island, a title achieved only after every other player dies? The short answer is: no one knows. If studies show no link between first-person, overtly graphic shooting games and real-life gun violence, then it is highly dubious that third-person cartoonified ones like *Fortnite* will ever be blamed. But what about the broader impact of the general message on increasingly younger minds? What about the imprinting? And the stimulation of the reward circuits? Clearly, I find myself unconvinced that gaming is *not* contributing at all to the epidemic of gun violence in our current culture.

In the end, like most other parents in America, I am furiously weighing the pros of violent video games against their cons, ultimately trying to tie them together with—or, better yet, completely divorce them from—the real-life gun violence epidemic. The vast majority of our sons will never pick up a gun and harm another person, shoot up a school, or even fantasize about any of it. The few who do face deep personal challenges and haven't figured out another way to resolve their anger, frustration, sadness, confusion, or whatever other emotional drivers exist. A profound lack of conflict resolution skills sits at the heart of this issue. Plus access to guns, access which is driven by an absurd numeric availability of firearms in this country and buoyed by a profound lack of laws regulating the sale, distribution, and use of these weapons. Failures across the board—like our lack of nationwide universal background checks, absent limits on the sale of military-style assault weapons and accessories, and inconsistent waiting period requirements across the states and no overarching federal waiting period requiremnt—have multiplied our gun violence crisis in the U.S.

In a culture seeing increased depression and anxiety, new research shows that a boy is more likely to carry a gun if he feels isolated, particularly if his parents disengage from him. This is totally distinct from the amount of time a parent might have with his or her child: whether we work or stay at home doesn't matter nearly as much as how present and connected we are when our kids are around. It's lack of warmth, communication, and connection that drives kids to feel isolated within their families. When this coexists with depression under a roof where there are accessible firearms, the combination can be deadly— yes, in a mass or school shooting scenario, but far more likely playing out through an act of suicide.

The bottom line is that males use guns overwhelmingly more than females. This trend starts young, but escalates rapidly through adolescence: when testosterone surges; when peer groups shift; when social media and gaming intensify; when their brains are mid-maturation and maximally imbalanced; and precisely when they go quiet with us. Gun violence should not be a rite of passage. But because we live in a society with a glut of firearms, we must talk about all of this—not just safe storage of weapons and desensitization to violent imagery (though we must talk about those!), but about coping strategies across the board so that our boys can manage their feelings without turning to deadly force. Talking has never been so important.

HOW TO TALK TO BOYS ABOUT ... GUNS AND GUN VIOLENCE

1. TALK ABOUT DEATH. Not a favorite topic for most, but the ultimate consequence of gun violence is loss of life. Younger kids may see an actor shot and killed

in one show just to reappear on another, confusing their notions of what it means to die. Older kids come to grips with mortality, but along the way many fear it so profoundly that they refuse to discuss it. Or they recognize the risks to others but not themselves. This is a massively heady topic. Take the opportunity to talk about it when you see images depicting gun violence, or hear news stories of shootings. The conversation can start with a prompt as simple as *What are you thinking?* when both you and your son watch, read, or witness the same thing.

2. REDUCE ANXIETY. School shooter drills might prepare kids for a hideous scenario, but they can also create profound fear. Know when your kids are having shooter drills at school—if the school doesn't inform parents, ask that they start doing so. This way, you can follow up afterward with questions like: *How did that drill feel? Do you have a plan if something were to happen? What steps do you think you can take in advance to prevent shootings in the first place?*

3. LIMIT ACCESS TO GUNS, AND EXPLAIN WHY. Regardless of where anyone stands on the gun ownership debate, it is nearly indisputable that access to firearms plus ammunition is a risk factor for youth gun violence. Talk about this. If you have a gun in your home, it needs to be unloaded and locked up. Ditto for family members and friends. Explain to your son why this is the right way to store a weapon—it's not an issue of trust, but rather one of safety.

4. GET HELP WHEN NEEDED. Suicide is the most common form of death by firearm in this country. So when you think there's something going on with your son, even just something small and trivial, ask him. Not just once, but regularly. *How are you doing? Who are you hanging out with? You seem down—is everything okay?* If he tells you he wants help, reach out to your pediatrician or a school counselor. If he denies a problem but your gut tells you there's something wrong, reach out as well. Beyond local health care providers, there exist a slew of good sites online pointing people to mental health resources and suicide prevention centers.

GETTING THEM OFF VIDEO GAMES

All video games impact our kids. Maybe not at first, and maybe not in the exact same way. But depending upon the game type—a spelling game likely won't cause the amp-up that a first-person-shooter game might—after enough time gaming on a screen, kids' behavior shifts. Some tips to stay ahead of the mood swing that often follows gaming:

1. FIGURE OUT YOUR KID'S MAGICAL NUM-BER. Most kids hit a mood wall after a fairly consistent amount of time. For some, that's half an hour; for others, it can be much longer. Try to get a clear sense of how long your son can stay on a device without transforming into an angry or short-tempered version of himself. And then stay ahead of that. Set a timer, give him a five-minute warning if he needs it, but do what you can to get him off before the mood switch.

2. SET GAMING RULES. In advance of video game play, set some rules, including the turn-off plan. And

then set some consequences, too, so that if he fights you when the time comes to be finished, you have pre-negotiated what will happen. The easiest consequence is simply taking away the game: If he has trouble getting off it, why would you want to let him back on?

3. GET GAMES OUT OF THE BEDROOM. It can be hard enough to convince your son to end a game. If he has access to them in his bedroom, he can go on—and stay on—at all hours. Important reminder here: most games flow easily across platforms these days, so keeping a phone in the bedroom overnight often equates to having 24/7 game access. All digital devices really should live outside of the bedroom.

4. IT'S NOT WORTH A REAL-LIFE BATTLE. If you find yourself fighting with your child endlessly over how to end video game play, just get rid of the games for a while. They're simply not worth the tradeoff. That means putting away gaming consoles, taking apps off phones and mobile devices, and double-checking that they're not hiding on laptops, too. Parental controls make these steps pretty easy: just search for a step-by-step video on how to use the parental controls on your devices. And don't miss the opportunity to explain to your son why you are suspending game play . . . or to point out the difference in his mood when he's off the games.

The End of My Lecture,
The Beginning of Your Conversation

After years of working in health care, teaching, and writing, I am ever more certain that talking is the key to health, wellness, and, yes, survival. Not just for our boys, but for everyone. Conversations with our sons will help them to survive and thrive, in the very same way they have empowered our daughters. An open dialogue now—even an awkward, stumbling, occasionally one-way conversation, be it about body changes, sex, drugs, or guns—can prepare and possibly protect our kids from future obstacles in life. But it must be a *real* dialogue, meaning that we put down our devices and our kids turn off theirs, too, acts that promote connection between people while reducing the (sometimes violent, sometimes beautiful and distracting) imagery on all of our screens, at least for a moment.

This book is peppered with talking tips, but ultimately your best strategy will reveal itself. Personality and circumstance dictate how people talk to one another, when, where, and with what intensity. Talking allows us to play out our thoughts with another person, to get their feedback, to reframe. It's the basis of all friendship and romance; as we make our way through the world, we are so often guided by others' voices in our minds. So why shouldn't talking be the basis of raising an adolescent, regardless of gender?

Ultimately, can talking directly impact the epidemic of gun violence? Or porn? Or body image struggles? Or any of the outside forces that affect our boys beginning in adolescence? I am certain the answer is yes. There's no downside to testing my theory.

THE DETAILS

THE BIOLOGY OF BOY PUBERTY— EVERYTHING GETS BIGGER

WELCOME TO THE INSIDE SCOOP ON what happens to boys' bodies when they go through puberty. In a nutshell, some things will get deeper, others greasier and smellier. And almost everything will get bigger.

Whether you are already an expert on body development, haven't quite mastered these topics, or if you just kinda sorta know some stuff, I encourage you to read on, because at some point during puberty, you will want to be able to explain to your son what the heck is happening to him. This overview is designed to cover the mechanics of his transformation into a man. But chances are it will also give you a window into your own boy, or at least a couple of *a-ha!* moments.

Before I dive into the details, though, a few major side notes about puberty. First, some people use the word "puberty" to describe a list of emerging physical characteristics; others a chemical cascade that results in these physical transformations and emotional changes. Throughout this book, I have gone with the latter, which means that puberty, at least as I (and most scientists I know) see it, starts without any great fanfare. That's because testosterone takes its sweet time metamorphosing boys into men.

The second big note is that once visible puberty begins, while there is a general order to things, there is no one right way to go through it. That means there's no predicting exactly what's going to happen, when, or how dramatically. The unpredictability of puberty is really the worst part. *Is he going to be an early bloomer or a late one? How bad will his acne be? When will his voice change? Precisely how many more years (or months or days) of growing does he have?* Unless your son is subjected to a slew of lab tests and X-rays, no one knows . . . and even then the answers are often vague. If anyone tells you otherwise, they're lying.

I start every puberty conversation—about boys and girls alike—with these notes of caution, because we live in a culture where being "normal" is reassuring and anything else potentially alienating, pathological, sometimes downright scary. So it's key to cut ourselves some slack when we are trying to figure out if puberty is proceeding "normally," since there's almost no such thing.

As you will read on the pages that follow, though, there is indeed a laundry list of things that will change over the course of many years. For sure, by the end of the process, your son will be able to put a check in every box. If I could only lay out a predictable list in chronological order of exactly what to expect and when . . . Turns out, puberty doesn't play that game. This fact is helpful for us as parents, but it's critical for our kids because adolescence is a time of wanting to conform or fit into a group (that is, until they want to rebel), and the unpredictability of puberty means that everyone going through it will experience some sense of being an outsider. Our kids—especially the tweens who are on the cusp of dramatic physical and emotional shifts, and the teens in the midst of them—want to know that what they see in the mirror and feel in their hearts (or guts or legs or groins) is okay.

And so, what follows is an alphabetical list of the body changes that will occur through puberty, with a relatively brief explanation of the behind-the-scenes biology. Since there's no absolute sequence to the appearance of these traits, there's also no systematic way to organize this information. A–Z is as reasonable as any other.

A note about why I left out the brain. Clearly, it is very much a part of the body and it changes dramatically during this time. But the brain is covered in great detail throughout this book, especially in Chapters 5 and 9, where it plays a starring role. So no need to try to boil down the brain's development into a handful of paragraphs when there's much more written elsewhere inside these pages.

Enough already. With no further ado, the boy puberty checklist:

ACNE

Zits, pimples, breakouts, whiteheads, blackheads. Whatever you want to call them, they are unwelcome eruptions on the skin's surface that can scar teenagers both physically and emotionally. Acne is a cruel injustice of this period in time, when the body is already in full revolt, and a common one at that, affecting about 85% of adolescents and young adults worldwide. Yes, you read that right: the vast majority of all kids on earth will break out.

Acne exists thanks to the teeny holes in our skin, commonly known as *pores*, or in medical lingo *pilosebaceous units* (PSUs). On the skin's surface, a PSU looks like a little pit, but it dives deep into the skin, taking the shape of a miniaturized long-neck chemistry flask. Within its rounded bottom, each PSU contains a hair follicle sprouting a hair (*pilo* = hair), an oil gland (*sebum* = human-produced oil), and a teeny-tiny muscle (which accounts for how your hairs can stand on end). We each have about five million PSUs spread over our entire body.

It is easy for a PSU to clog, especially during puberty. That's because it is lined with cells that multiply when hormones surge in the tween and teen years. A PSU's long neck can quickly clog with proliferating cells, like a cork in a wine bottle.

Meanwhile, at the roomy bottom of the pore, the hair follicle continues to grow and the oil gland secretes its oil. Almost inevitably this greasy, sludgy sebum mix becomes trapped by the cell-plug, sometimes along with a hair that has curled in on itself.

Once a PSU is plugged and congested with oily backup, oxygen cannot reach its rounded base. And thanks to that, certain bacteria that thrive in the absence of oxygen begin to grow down at the bottom of the pore, the most common of which is called *Propionibacterium acnes*. These bacteria feed off human oils, multiply, feed more furiously, and multiply even faster, generally having a grand old time. At a certain point, between the oil and the cells and the bacteria and the hair, there is so much congestion that the plugged PSU will burst. Sometimes it erupts outward like a mini-volcano on the surface of the skin, but most of the time the rupture happens at the bottom of the pore, the PSU's base giving out like your overfilled kitchen trash bag. The body's immune system then swoops into action, attempting to clean up the mess. This line of defense causes inflammation in the PSU and sometimes redness and swelling on the skin. So if you are wondering why some zits look angrier than others, even on the same face, you now know that it just depends upon whether or not the immune system has been fully activated.

If you want to have something to blame for the existence of acne in the first place, blame the hormones that govern much of puberty, like androgens. When levels of androgen rise in the blood, so too does oil production in the PSU. But most researchers think that it's not solely the existence of new hormones coursing through the bloodstream during puberty that causes acne; rather, it's their rise and fall. Until hormone surges mellow out later in adolescence, their levels can swing quite wildly, and it's this swing that results in zits.

Acne indignantly appears on the most visible parts of the body: the face, neck, upper chest, and upper back (the joking name for the last is "backne" . . . but the same hormones that cause it may also predispose your kid to find the term highly unamusing). Regardless of where it crops up, acne often responds to a good skin-cleansing routine. That's because a gentle cleanser or non-irritating soap can wash away the cell-plug at the top of the PSU. Cleansing is a good start, but many kids will also need to treat their skin with products containing benzoyl peroxide or retinol (or both) to address what's going on deeper in the PSU. These products have antibacterial and anti-inflammatory properties, and can work wonders for teens and adults alike. For those with more severe acne, there are antibiotics to eradicate those pesky *Propionibacterium acnes*, vitamin-A derivatives to target sebum production and inflammation, and other treatments available by prescription.

As the hormone surges of puberty settle down, so too does acne. It doesn't go away for everyone; many adults can attest to having zits for decades. But the peak of acne badness occurs around age fifteen for both sexes, and tends to diminish as puberty ends its run. The reason acne sticks with us well beyond our teen years has to do with the fact that sex hormones continue to vacillate throughout our reproductive lives. Other hormones, like insulin and IGF-1, play a role too, which is why even though androgens start to find a more regular level by the late teens, many other hormones in the body don't necessarily follow the same pattern* . . . and that explains acne's endless appearance throughout life.

---

* Estrogen is thought to offset the oil-producing effects of androgen. This is why women often have breakouts just before they get their periods: as their estrogen levels drop, the uterine lining begins to shed and at the same time the effect of circulating androgens goes unchecked. Likewise, women who take oral contraceptive pills (OCPs), particularly ones with estrogen, often see improvements in their skin. This is because OCPs deliver steady levels of hormone to the body, reducing the fluctuations that are associated with breakouts.

3 WAYS TO MINIMIZE PIMPLE FORMATION (THIS WILL WORK FOR YOUR SON . . . AND FOR YOU, TOO):

1. WASH THE FACE in the morning and at night. Washing more frequently than that won't help, and often creates its own problems. Use a gentle cleanser or soap without colors, perfumes, or alcohols. Side note: Don't over-dry the skin, or the oil glands will think they need to produce more moisture, causing rebound breakouts. So follow cleansing with a moisturizer or sunscreen/moisturizer combination.

2. AVOID TRIGGERING THE ADRENAL GLANDS, which have the dual task of making androgen and acting as the center of our stress response, a process highly associated with inflammation. Remember, anything that causes androgens to seesaw or inflammatory cells to swarm can begin a chain reaction that ultimately affects our skin. This means that breakouts can be caused, at least indirectly, by everything from stress to poor sleep to a high-sugar diet. The best way to keep skin looking good, then, is old-fashioned clean living: drink lots of water; sleep enough hours at night; eat a diet heavy on whole foods and minimalist on processed or sugary ones; reduce stressors; keep known toxins and irritants out of and off your body. Basically, treat yourself—and your adrenal glands—with respect.

3. KEEP THE HANDS OFF THE FACE! While picking skin doesn't cause acne, it sure does increase inflammation, risk for infection, and eventual scarring.

BODY ODOR

When the body gets overheated, the sweat glands bathe the skin with moisture to cool it off—making sweating a very elegant system, despite the pit stains. But when we sweat, eventually we smell. This is true for people of all ages. The thing is, kids heading into puberty suddenly sweat a whole lot more than they used to.

Sweat itself is usually odorless. But our bodies have two types of sweat glands, one more likely to result in a stinky odor than the other. *Eccrine* sweat glands are scattered all over and produce sweat made mostly of water. *Apocrine* sweat glands are concentrated in the hairy spots (the scalp, armpits, and groin) and a few other places where the skin folds over on itself and the sun doesn't shine (like belly button, anus, and ears). These glands make sweat containing fatty acids, proteins, and by-products like ammonium and urea. The proteins in apocrine sweat are particularly yummy for bacteria, and in case you didn't know, we all have bacteria living on our skin. So when our apocrine sweat glands get busy working to cool us down, they also produce a culinary feast for the bacteria hanging around; and when these bacteria consume the proteins within the sweat, the breakdown product is an acid with a distinct odor, unique to each person depending upon the types and numbers of bacteria on the skin, the balance of proteins in the sweat, and so on. But not so unique that we don't all recognize it as stink. I have yet to meet a person whose sweat smells like roses.

Kids start to generate body odor during puberty because that's when their apocrine glands get more active (thank you, androgens!). In fact, one of the most common early signs of puberty tends to be increasing quantities of sweat. Remember, there's no absolute right order to how puberty flows, so this may not be the case for your kid. But generally speaking, by the fifth grade, most teachers are making a plea to their students to start wearing some deodorant.

Speaking of deodorant, a quick crash course in how anti-B.O.

products work. Deodorant de-odorizes. It kills the bacteria on the skin—it doesn't wipe them out completely, but it gets rid of enough of them that when the protein-rich sweat comes their way, there aren't enough bacteria left to generate stench-producing levels of acid. The bacteria repopulate pretty quickly, though, which accounts for why deodorants need to be applied daily in order to work. Antiperspirants are anti-perspiration, so they stop sweat production. Again, not entirely, but enough so that the protein load being offered to the local bacteria is small—it's a snack, not a three-course meal. This means that when bacteria digest the lesser volume of proteins, they release a smaller amount of stinky acid. Most products on drugstore shelves are combination antiperspirant-plus-deodorant, because attacking both sides of the equation works best.

You know what doesn't work? Trying to cover up the sweat smell with a stronger smell (adolescent boys seem to think simply spraying on an Axe (or Lynx) product is a winning strategy—news flash: it's not). Another B.O. prevention fail is to shower without soap. The reason bathing makes us smell better is that we use soap to remove the bacteria, proteins, and acids on our skin. Standing under some running water without actively washing away these culprits accomplishes very little.

Many people claim they cannot smell their own body odor, and to some extent it's true. Walking around, we don't tend to register our own subtle smells, good or bad, as easily as we recognize those of others. That said, it's not difficult to take a whiff of one's own armpit to discover what others may have already surmised. Teach your son that simple self-check, and it will pay off in hygiene spades.

3 WAYS TO MINIMIZE BODY ODOR (THESE WORK FOR EVERYONE, NOT JUST PUBESCENT BOYS!):

1. SHOWER WITH SOAP. Or bathe with soap. Or on those days where there isn't time or access to a bath or shower, sponge bathe the stinky spots . . . with soap! Soap reduces the bacterial load and the lingering acids on the skin.

2. DEODORIZE WHERE YOU CAN. Some families opt to use store-bought antiperspirants and deodorants; others have strong feelings about the ingredients in these products. Choose products that work for your family, but remember to stay away from ones containing perfumes and colors, as these can irritate the skin. And just because a container has the word "natural" on it, this doesn't mean the product inside is any safer or healthier for you. Natural means nothing in the world of cosmetics.*

3. AIR THINGS OUT. There are lots of spots on the body that aren't designed to be covered in antiperspirant or deodorant (most, actually). The ones that tend to get stinkiest are the areas wrapped in tight clothing, because these spots sweat more. Think: feet and groin. Here, air is the antidote. At the end of the day, have your son remove his shoes and socks (you may need to clear out for a few minutes—that smell can be strong) and wear flip-flops, slides, or just go barefoot inside.

---

* Really, the word "natural" has no value on a label. I could call the page you are reading right now "natural," and the chair you are sitting in, pen you are writing with, and cup you are drinking from too. This is a major pet peeve of most health care folks I know, from doctors and nurses to nutritionists and public health advocates. So, beware of falling into this trap when cruising the aisles of the grocery store . . .

And at night, sleeping in loose-fitting underwear or none at all allows air to circulate in the groin.

ERECTIONS

They've been happening since your son was a baby, but suddenly erections can be a big deal. That's partly because the penis is bigger, so they're more noticeable. It's also a function of frequency: starting in puberty, erections seem to happen all the time (which isn't exactly true, but given that the average man has about eleven of them during the day, and another four or five at night, it can feel that way).

Some basics. Even though the slang for erection is "boner," there's no bone in the penis. An erection occurs when blood fills the two long pieces of spongy tissue, called the *corpora cavernosa,* that run down the shaft on either side of the *urethra* (the tube that carries urine from the bladder to the tip of the penis; the same tube that will eventually carry semen in pubescent and post-pubescent males). During an erection, the tiny muscles inside the corpora cavernosa relax, allowing the tissue to collect more blood than it drains. This blood is temporarily trapped by a membrane covering the corpora cavernosa called the *tunica albuginea,* which further increases pressure in the tissue. The shaft of the penis engorges, stiffens, and stays that way until the muscles of the corpora cavernosa constrict again, causing blood to flow out.

There is such a thing as a "penile fracture," but with no bone, there's nothing to fracture, exactly, so the term only exists because it was invented a century ago and has stuck around. Really a penile fracture is a tear in the tunica albuginea. The penis must be erect for this to occur, and the recipient of some sort of blunt trauma (forceful sex, really aggressive masturbation, or an injury like rolling over onto an erect penis, falling onto it, or forcing it into tight pants—I am not making any of this up; even though it's super rare to break a penis after a fall or roll, it's all reported in the medical literature).[*]

Guys get erections because they have sexual feelings and thoughts, notions that debut during puberty. They get erections during sleep, too, though usually only in deeper REM sleep cycles. And most guys report waking up with an erection often, if not every day. Guys also get spontaneous erections for no apparent reason at all, and they can even get reflex erections, which happen with stress, nervousness, fear, or anger (basically, the opposite of sexy thoughts). Whenever I am teaching girls about their bodies and they complain that thanks to periods they drew the physiological short straw, I tell them about spontaneous and reflex erections. Suddenly they don't feel so sorry for themselves.

3 WAYS TO MANAGE AN INCONVENIENT ERECTION:

1. SIT, DON'T STAND, at least if you can, so no one notices.

2. HANDS IN THE POCKETS. This just makes the front of the pants look slightly bigger, concealing the fact that something's sticking out.

3. WEAR TIGHTER-FITTING UNDERPANTS. In general, underwear fit should be a completely personal prefer-

---

[*] These and other, wilder explanations of penile fracture (a falling brick smashing the penis is surprisingly not uncommon) appear all over the Internet, from blogs to medical journals. Let's take a moment to ask why stories like this continue to show up basically everywhere. Because there's no way falling off of a mountain onto an erect penis (yes, officially reported) is a cautionary tale we need to teach our sons. These "data" remind us that sex is a taboo topic all over the world, and men feel compelled to exaggerate or lie to their health care providers about what precisely they were doing when they injured their family jewels.

ence, and there's a strong argument for loose-fitting boxers given the comments in the body odor section above. But the looser the fit, the more room for movement. So if inconvenient erections are a recurring issue, try a slightly tighter fit, like a boxer brief or classic brief. That said, not *too* tight, because too much compression can be uncomfortable—not to mention the source of chafing and irritation.

(What? No comment here about redirecting thoughts away from a crush and focusing instead on baseball stats or Grandma's favorite recipe? If the erection is caused by a sexy thought, then yes, pivot your thoughts and it should help. But since erections often come up for no apparent reason, trying to neutralize what's running through your mind often doesn't solve the issue.)

GROWTH SPURTS

If you ever want to motivate your kid to get into bed, just repeat the truism: *You grow when you sleep.* Because that's exactly what happens. During the body's downtime, so long as the growth plates are still open for business, the bones have the opportunity to elongate. What's actually happening is that the pituitary gland inside the brain—the same gland responsible for releasing LH and FSH to message the testes in boys and the ovaries in girls, and also the same gland that sends thyroid-stimulating hormone to the thyroid to rule energy management—makes *growth hormone* (GH). During deep sleep, GH leaves the pituitary in pulses, messaging the body's bones to grow. GH controls much more than just growth: it's responsible for the overall homeostasis of many of our organs and tissues, which is why all of us still have it hanging around even though, as adults, we are on a slow height decline. But in adolescence, it plays a major role in how big a kid will become.

Now, there's growing and there's GROWING. The famous adolescent growth spurt represents growth in every long bone of the skeleton (and many of the smaller bones, too) at a rate 50%–100% faster than regular kid growth. The growth spurt typically lasts a couple of years, but sometimes goes on much longer. When it's done, growth doesn't halt altogether—most kids actually eke out an extra inch (or several) before the growth plates fuse and final height is achieved. And while there's some controversy about exactly how much direct control GH has over the whole process, its levels double during the spurt, evidence that it plays a central role.

Adolescence isn't the first time kids experience a serious growth spurt. Between birth and turning one, a typical baby grows ten inches (I have seen many grow more than a foot) and birthweight triples (I've seen much more than that, too). Then the process slows to a more rational pace for several years. As for when it will begin again, the answer is highly individual. On average, girls start their growth spurt around age ten and boys at eleven or twelve, helping to explain why the beginning of middle school is often marked by females towering over their male classmates. But like everything else in puberty, the timing of growth spurt onset is unpredictable, and so too is its duration: while growth spurts for boys tend to last up to a year longer than for girls (explaining why the average adult male is several inches taller than the average adult female), again this all depends.

Genetics play a large role in a person's ultimate height. The best guess for how tall a child will become is the mid-parental height equation, where a kid's estimated height is the answer to the following equation, plus or minus two inches. All the heights in these equations are measured in inches.

$$\text{FOR BOYS: } \frac{(\text{genetic mom's height} + 5) + \text{genetic dad's height}}{2}$$

$$\text{FOR GIRLS: } \frac{\text{genetic mom's height} + (\text{genetic dad's height} - 5)}{2}$$

A word of caution about body predictions in general and height in particular: while the mid-parental height equation represents what happens for the majority of people, there is a constant stream of kids for whom it will be completely off. Sometimes an underlying medical issue is to blame; sometimes poor nutrition or environmental stress. And sometimes it's simply the existence of a random outlier relative—the 6'3" aunt you've never met or the storied 4'11" great-great-great-grandfather, whose genes trickle their way down the family tree and voilà!—a kid turns out to be much shorter or taller than anticipated.

3 WAYS TO MAXIMIZE GROWTH (BECAUSE ALMOST EVERY KID I HAVE EVER MET ASKS ME THIS QUESTION):

1. SLEEP WELL! Both the quantity and quality of sleep matter for growth. Things like a regular bedtime routine and a reasonable lights-out time are important, but so too is having a safe, comfortable place to sleep.

2. EAT WELL! My son grew nearly a foot over the course of two years. I watched him eat everything in sight. From a weight perspective, it probably wouldn't have mattered if he consumed a few extra junk foods, but in terms of health and wellness both short- and long-term, the quality of food makes a massive difference. Plus, good habit formation is key to lifelong wellness.

3. DON'T STRESS. Much easier said than done . . . but growth happens when it happens and, if nutrition and sleep are in order, there isn't too much else to do. When we worry less, we usually sleep and eat better. See the cycle? So talk to a doctor—preferably a pediatrician or a pediatric endocrinologist—if there are questions about worrisome growth patterns, but otherwise just be patient.

HAIR, HAIR, EVERYWHERE

Hair growth certainly happens during puberty, but it's not a symptom of the process. This is explained in some detail in Chapter 2, but bears repeating briefly here.

The appearance of hair, hair, everywhere—all new pubic, armpit, and eventually facial hair, but also thickening arm and leg hair—falls under the banner of *adrenarche,* because it is governed by the hormones released from the adrenal glands. To quote Louise Greenspan, author of *The New Puberty,* "Adrenarche is not puberty!!" (the exclamation points are Louise's— she literally said, "add exclamation points!"). What she means is this: puberty is governed by testosterone in boys and estrogen in girls, plus a handful of other hormones too, resulting in sexual maturity and the ability to reproduce. Adrenarche might plant the seeds of hair growth, but it doesn't lead to baby-making potential. So, while parents and kids alike often think that when hair begins to appear this is a sign of starting puberty, now you know it's not. Others think that without hair, he's not really in it—that's untrue as well. Adrenarche and puberty run on parallel paths, often perfectly in sync but not always.

Pubic and armpit hair tend to emerge around the same time, or at least within several months of each other. That said, the hair in one spot may be very thin, almost invisible, while the hair in the other might be thick and curly from the get-go. And there are certainly guys who have hair down there way before the armpit fuzz appears, or vice versa. Facial hair starts with a thin mustache growing close to the top lip. Now mind you, there are guys who have had a thin mustache since preschool, but even those kids will see thickening here before anything else on the face. Over time, the eyebrows become fuller, sideburns grow lower, and eventually (usually years later) the beard appears. All the while, leg and arm hair coarsen, followed by chest hair poking out, initially in the central triangle between the collarbone and the two nipples, but eventually (again, usually years later) across the rest of the chest, the abdomen, and yes, even on the back.

Hair does serve a purpose for humans, which is why we grow more of it as we approach adulthood, though not nearly as much as our ape relatives. The hairs on our body keep us warm when our baby fat melts away; in our nostrils and ears, hairs protect us from dirt and germs. There's no consensus yet on why the heck we sprout armpit and pubic hair, though theories include an extra line of defense for the immune system and trapping scents that attract others. (While I understand the evolutionary thinking, still that last idea seems like a bit of a stretch.)

3 HAIR CARE STRATEGIES (THAT ARE TRUE FOR ALL OF US):

1. IF HE WANTS TO START SHAVING, HELP HIM OUT. There is no mandate to shave the mustache and beard. In fact, these days many guys live by the mantra *if you've got it, flaunt it*. But if shaving is desired, guys need to learn how to use razors safely and effectively. A couple of basics: never shave dry with a straight razor; don't shave wet with an electric shaver (unless it's designed to handle that); and never, ever use a blade that looks old or rusty.

2. SKIN PREP IS KEY. Shaving works best when the skin is warm and slightly damp, so either shave after a shower or prep the skin first with a warm-water face wash. Always shave a clean face, meaning one that's dirt-free. As for soaps, gels, and shaving creams, those will vary depending upon the type of razor being used and personal preference.

3. HAIRS CAN LOSE THEIR SENSE OF DIRECTION. Sometimes, instead of poking out through the skin, they can get coiled underneath. This is especially common for curly hairs, and when it happens the follicle may become inflamed. What might look like a pimple is actually an ingrown hair. Don't pick at it! If a whole crop pops up, your son may need some help from a dermatologist. The best home-prevention strategy for ingrowns: wash hairy areas with soap on a washcloth or even a gentle loofah, to help lift off dead skin cells that block the hairs' way to the skin surface.

MOODS

Classic puberty moodiness is female, right? Wrong. Boys get moody too, they just swing in different directions. Of course, I am completely generalizing about how they swing here, because every child is different and yours may not follow these patterns. But since common things are common, as we like to say in medicine, it's worthwhile to address trends.

The hormonal surges of puberty—particularly the ups and downs of testosterone—impact the entire body. Thanks to the circulatory system, blood goes round and round, and the brain is exposed to hormone peaks and troughs just like everything below the neck. There isn't a ton of science connecting precisely which puberty-steering hormones or other chemicals produced by the body impact which parts of the brain. But here's what we do know: around the same time that testosterone makes its debut, so too do boy moods. Some get quiet or withdraw; others become more impulsive or aggressive or even angry; most have some combination of the two, with long spells of their baseline sweet, normal selves in between. And a few guys don't swing one bit, remaining as evenly keeled as they always have been, just as they were way before their testicles ever enlarged.

Moodiness is mentioned all over this book, especially in Chapters 2 and 5. But because I have never met a kid who likes how it feels to be moody, it bears mentioning again here. Emotional swings during puberty are completely normal, as are swings before puberty starts and long after it's done. But feelings ranging from wanting to shut the world out to the urge to jump into something headfirst without looking tend to happen concurrent with body transformation, so commonly that I think they deserve to be listed as official signs of puberty.

3 WAYS TO MANAGE MOOD SWINGS (THESE WORK FOR PEOPLE OF ALL AGES):

1. TAKE A BREATH. Count to ten. Walk away for a minute. As you feel yourself slipping toward a mood—or even once you are squarely in it—taking a mental or physical break can help us reset.

2. PLAN AHEAD for what to do when a mood strikes. We don't always have to think on our feet. When there's an opportunity to consider a situation ahead of time, we almost always handle it better. This is why role-playing works.

3. APOLOGIZE to others and to yourself. We are never our best selves in the midst of a mood swing, so if you

owe someone an apology, give it. And then give yourself a break, because we are often better at forgiving
others than ourselves.

VOICE CHANGES

The voice deepens for everyone going through puberty, boys
and girls alike. But among girls the pitch change is often quite
subtle, whereas in boys . . . not so much.

Voice changes result from growth of the *larynx*. The larynx is
a tube made up of small muscles, ligaments, and cartilage. It
sits inside the neck on top of the *trachea*, the main airway leading to the lungs. Given its position, the larynx plays a number of
critical roles: it protects the airway by closing before anything
that's not supposed to go down that way has the chance (like
food, for instance); it plays a role in breathing and coughing;
and it is responsible for how we make sounds. This last job
earned the larynx its nickname: the voice box.

During puberty, testosterone stimulates the larynx to grow. It
also causes the *vocal cords*—small muscles that lie across the
top of the larynx—to stretch and thicken. When air pushes up
from the lungs through the larynx and across the vocal cords,
they vibrate, generating sound. Because of the changes in the
shape of the larynx and vocal cords during puberty, the vibra-
tions shift as well, lowering the pitch of the sounds. This doesn't
happen seamlessly, though: as the structures are growing and
thickening, a guy can be surprised by squeaks and cracks in his
voice. Usually, within months the voice settles down and those
unanticipated sounds disappear.

Because testosterone impacts the overall growth of the larynx, and because the larynx sits in the neck, just beneath the
skin's surface, physical changes here can be quite noticeable,
especially in the cartilage along the front-facing part of the larynx. Nicknamed the Adam's apple (apparently a tribute to the
biblical Adam getting a piece of the fruit lodged in his throat),

this structure can be seen bobbing up and down in some necks starting mid-puberty.

It's worth noting that testosterone isn't the only hormone to impact the larynx: estrogen and progesterone do as well. But their effect is less dramatic, which explains why the downward shift in vocal pitch is far less noticeable for girls than for boys.

3 WAYS TO MANAGE VOCAL CHANGES:

1. **WHEN THE VOICE CRACKS OR SQUEAKS, BARREL THROUGH** as if nothing has happened. Much of the time, no one else really notices anyhow. This can be trickier for guys who sing, so if that's you, ask other performers or teachers for some recommendations here.

2. **SEE THE LIGHT AT THE END OF THE TUNNEL.** This is a short-term issue. There is no medicine to take, lozenge to suck on, or drink to swallow that will make it go away. But rest assured that in just a few weeks or months, the problem will be solved.

3. **OWN YOUR NEW VOICE.** One of the most common refrains a guy will hear—almost always from an adult who hasn't seen him in a while—is *Oh my gosh! Your voice is so deep!* This can be embarrassing to some, annoying to others. Come up with a great response that makes you comfortable, because if you've heard it once, you will almost certainly hear it again. One easy reply is a simple: *Yup.*

WET DREAMS

If the whole point of puberty is to reach reproductive maturity, then wet dreams are a sign of being well on the way. A wet dream (aka *nocturnal emission*) happens during sleep when *semen,* a mixture of sperm and the fluids produced in and around the testicles, is ejaculated unbeknownst to the guy until he wakes up the next morning to find a wet spot on his bed. So when a boy starts having wet dreams, there's evidence that his body is becoming reproductively mature.

Many guys think the wet spot is urine (it's not). And lots of them, at least the first few times it happens, are embarrassed by having had a wet dream (but they generally get over that). Most of them find it helpful to know that there's a difference between wet dreams and masturbation, which boils down to conscious-ness: *masturbation* is sexual self-pleasure often resulting in or-gasm with ejaculation; a wet dream happens during sleep, with no known self-pleasuring.

Wet dreams are reported as being fairly common, occurring in up to 80% of guys. But this isn't exactly a burgeoning field of research—it's neither an area of medical concern nor one for which tween and teen boys are eagerly volunteering themselves for a study—so 80% may be a huge over- or underestimation. Lots of men say they have never had a wet dream in their life. For those who have, there's a wide range of frequency, anywhere from a couple of times per week to once every few months. Again, not much data is being collected here, so it's hard to say what guys should anticipate. The bottom line is that wet dreams are nor-mal, and not having wet dreams is normal too.

3 THINGS TO DO IF YOU'VE HAD A WET DREAM (ADVICE FOR THE GUYS):

1. CLEAN UP. Since someone has to clean off the sheets, it really should be the one who made the mess. And it's no big deal, since the spot from a wet dream is generally quite small and usually wipes away with a damp cloth.

2. FEEL NO SHAME IF YOU HAVE ONE. Wet dreams are completely normal and not a sign of anything bad or wrong.

3. FEEL NO SHAME IF YOU DON'T HAVE ONE. Because that's completely normal, too.

Acknowledgments

MY MOM HAMMERED INTO ME THE value of the thank-you note, which is why, I suppose, I loved writing this acknowledgments section. To that end, I will start by thanking family. They often get saved for last in this part of a book (in that save-the-best-for-last kind of way), but since they are so primary to everything I do, I wanted to put them first here. To Paul, my husband, my rock, my copy editor, my brain trust, and the kindest soul on the planet (according to pretty much everyone who has ever met you) . . . If every boy on earth could grow up to be the type of man you are, the world would be a better place. Thank you for keeping everything real for me, for creating the space I need so I can do this work, and for writing me little notes of encouragement when you know I need them. Plus correcting me from time to time about what it's like to be male. And to our two kids, Talia and Ry . . . Even though I will never know what it is to parent any other children, I know with certainty the love couldn't run deeper, the laughs couldn't be bigger, and the pride couldn't fill my heart any more. It's not easy growing up with a mom who teaches and writes about puberty for a living. You two do it with grace and ease, and without realizing that you are my most invaluable teachers.

Thank you to my mom for the whole thank-you note imprinting, but also for the endless love, not to mention PR; and to my three brothers—Greg, Anthony, and Seth, the first boys I ever decoded—for the inspiration not to mention life lessons (but not for the noogies, guys). To Joe, Idell, Barb and Zach, Amy and Steve, Cyd, and Rem, you embody the best in-law situation imaginable, where every family dinner is equal parts encouragement and intellectual rigor. (It's more fun than it sounds.)

Over the past ten years, I have written cartoonified health manuals for kids. There is no room for acknowledgments in those, not even a one-line dedication. So while there are many folks to be thanked for helping with *Decoding Boys*, it all really started with Barbara Stretchberry, my American Girl editor and sidekick since 2011. Without Barbara, the *Care and Keeping* series would have looked a whole lot different, and I am quite convinced there would be no *Guy Stuff*. Without that last book, I don't think this one would exist either. A few other belated thanks as well to the entire Mattel and American Girl team, including but definitely not limited to Carrie Anton, Ellen Brothers, Stephanie Cota, Jodi Goldberg, Susan Jevens, Darcie Johnson, Jean McKenzie, Julie Parks, Julia Prohaska, Tammie Scadden, and Stephanie Spanos. Some of you are still at AG, others have moved on—all of you were invaluable along my journey.

And now, on to the present day. Marnie Cochran and Heather Jackson, you are the dynamic duo of editing and agenting. I really didn't know at the outset I was signing up for a team sport. How lucky I was! Thank you for your edits, comments, thoughts, pushback, and support, all perfectly balanced. To the entire Ballantine team, for trusting my instincts and educating me with your expertise—from the first time we sat around a table together I recognized my good fortune. And to the load of folks along the way who read chapters, made themselves available for interviews, answered emails, and opened their brains for the picking: Anisha Abraham, Vanessa Bennett, Catherine Caccialanza, Yee-Ming Chan, Mallika Chopra, Aleksandra Crapanzano, Jonathan Crystal, Embeth Davidtz, Gail Dines, David Eisenman, Heather Fullerton, Michele Gathrid, Andrew Goldberg, Louise Greenspan, Nalin Gupta, Marcia Herman-Giddens, Nick Kroll, Michael Levin, Alison Locker, Andrea Nevins, Katherine Peabody, Michelle Sandberg, Dan Siegel, Jeannie Suk Gerson, Yalda Uhls, Emma Watts, and Adam Winkler. A special shout-out to Steve Silvestro for the phrase "Everything Gets Bigger."

Ultimately, I wouldn't have had anything to say without the wise kids who open up when I begin to ask questions about life during puberty. Thanks to every guy—and girl—I have ever cared for in the office, taught in a classroom, or interviewed on the subject. Your honesty helps move the needle for parents everywhere. I feel so fortunate that you spoke openly with me . . . hopefully this book will be the start of lots more conversations.

Bibliography

ENCLOSED IS A LIST OF RESOURCES, books, articles, and websites that proved invaluable to the writing of this book. But for some chapters, the cited works list is thin. That is because this book is a result of twenty years as a pediatrician, ten years as a dedicated writer and speaker, and therefore countless conversations, queries, interviews, and searches on each of these topics. I wish I had kept a running log of every resource I have used to build my knowledge, but I haven't. So here are the specifics that I relied upon for this book, built upon half a lifetime of learning.

CHAPTER TWO: UNDERSTANDING TESTOSTERONE

Duke, Sally Anne, Ben W. R. Balzer, and Katharine S. Steinbeck. "Testosterone and Its Effects on Human Male Adolescent Mood and Behavior: A Systematic Review," *Journal of Adolescent Health*, vol. 55, no. 3 (2014): 315–22.

Fleming, Amy. "Does Testosterone Make You Mean?" *The Guardian* (U.S. edition), March 20, 2018.

Peper, Jiska S., P. Cédric M. P. Koolschijn, and Eveline A. Crone. "Development of Risk Taking: Contributions from Adolescent Testosterone and the Orbito-Frontal Cortex," *Journal of Cognitive Neuroscience*, vol. 25, no. 12 (2013): 2141–50.

Piekarski, David J., et al. "Does Puberty Mark a Transition in Sensitive Periods for Plasticity in the Associative Neocortex?" *Brain Research*, vol. 1654, Part B (2017): 123–44.

Rosenfield, Robert L. "Normal Adrenarche," Up To Date, https://www .uptodate.com/contents/normal-adrenarche#subscribeMessage.

Parry, Vivenne. *The Truth About Hormones* (London: Atlantic Books, 2009).

CHAPTER THREE: YES, YOUR NINE-YEAR-OLD MIGHT BE IN PUBERTY

Biro, F. M., et al. "Pubertal Assessment Method and Baseline Characteristics in a Mixed Longitudinal Study of Girls," *Pediatrics*, vol. 126, no. 3 (2010): e583-90. DOI: 10.1542/peds.2009-3079.

Euling, Susan Y., et al. "Examination of US Puberty-Timing Data from 1940 to 1994 for Secular Trends: Panel Findings," *Pediatrics*, vol. 121, Supplement 3 (2008): s172–91.

Greenspan, Louise, and Julianna Deardorff. *The New Puberty* (New York: Rodale, 2014).

Herman-Giddens, Marcia E., et al. "Secondary Sexual Characteristics and Menses in Young Girls Seen in Office Practice: A Study from the Pediatric Research in Office Settings Network," *Pediatrics*, vol. 99, no. 4 (1997): 505–12.

———. "Secondary Sexual Characteristics in Boys: Data from the Pediatric Research in Office Settings Network," *Pediatrics*, vol. 130, no. 5 (2012): e1058–68.

Marshall, W. A., and J. M Tanner. "Variations in Pattern of Pubertal Changes in Girls," *Archives of Diseases in Childhood*, vol. 44, no. 235 (1969): 291–303.

CHAPTER FOUR: LATER, DUDE

Kulin, Howard. "Extensive Personal Experience: Delayed Puberty," *Journal of Clinical Endocrinology and Metabolism*, vol. 81, no. 10 (1996): 3460–64.

MacDonald, Alec. "5 Awkward Struggles for Guys Who Hit Puberty Too Late in Life," *EliteDaily.com*, July 23, 2015, https://www.elitedaily.com/humor/ puberty-too-late-in-life/1136669.

Niles, Robert. "Standard Deviation," RobertNiles.com, accessed May 10, 2019, https://www.robertniles.com/stats/stdev.shtml.

Palmert, Mark R., and Leo Dunkel. "Delayed Puberty," *New England Journal of Medicine*, vol. 366 (2012): 443–53. DOI: 10.1056/NEJMcp1109290.

Pitteloud, Nelly. "Managing Delayed or Altered Puberty in Boys," *BMJ*, vol. 345 (2012): e7913. DOI: 10.1136/bmj.e7913.

Zhu, Jia, and Chan, Yee-Ming. "Adult Consequences of Self-Limited Delayed Puberty," *Pediatrics*, vol. 139, no. 6 (217): e20163177.

CHAPTER FIVE: WHEN THEY LOOK LIKE ADULTS BUT DON'T THINK LIKE THEM

Bailey, Regina. "The Limbic System of the Brain," ThoughtCo.com, March 28, 2018, https://www.thoughtco.com/limbic-system-anatomy-373200.

Giedd, Jay N. "The Teen Brain: Primed to Learn, Primed to Take Risks," *The Dana Foundation*, February 26, 2009, dana.org/article/the-teen-brain-primed-to-learn-primed-to-take-risks/.

Paredes, Mercedes F., et al. "Extensive Migration of Young Neurons into the Infant Human Frontal Lobe," *Science*, vol. 354, no. 6308 (2016). DOI: 10.1126/science.aaf7073.

Piekarski, D. J., et al. "Does Puberty Mark a Transition in Sensitive Periods for Plasticity in the Associative Neocortex?" *Brain Research*, vol. 1654, Part B (2017): 123–44.

Shen, Helen. "Does the Adult Brain Really Grow New Neurons?" *Scientific American*, March 7, 2018, https://www.scientificamerican.com/article/does-the-adult-brain-really-grow-new-neurons/.

Sorrells, Shawn F., et al. "Human Hippocampal Neurogenesis Drops Sharply in Children to Undetectable Levels in Adults," *Nature*, vol. 555 (2018): 377–83.

Stiles, Joan, and Terry L. Jernigan. "The Basics of Brain Development," *Neuropsychology Review*, vol. 20, no. 4 (2010): 327–48.

Suleiman, Ahna Ballonoff, and Ronald E. Dahl. "Leveraging Neuroscience to Inform Adolescent Health: The Need for an Innovative Transdisciplinary Developmental Science of Adolescence," *Journal of Adolescent Health*, vol. 60, no. 3 (2017): 240–48.

CHAPTER SIX: BOYS AND "THE TALK"

Green, Laci. "Laci Green: Sex Ed for the Internet," Lacigreen.tv, accessed May 10, 2019.

Hess, Amanda. "The Sex Ed Queens of YouTube Don't Need a PhD," *New York Times*, September 30, 2016.

Sweeney, Julia. "Julia Sweeney Has 'The Talk,'" TED.com, February 2010, https://www.ted.com/talks/julia_sweeney_has_the_talk?language=en.

Vagianos, Alanna. "Laci Green on Her New MTV Series and Dealing with Backlash as a Feminist on the Internet," *Huffington Post*, November 26, 2014, https://www.huffingtonpost.com/2014/11/26/laci-green-mtv-braless-youtube_n_6214632.html.

CHAPTER SEVEN: BOYS AND SEX

Culture Reframed. Culturereframed.org, accessed May 10, 2019.

Enough Is Enough. "Statistics: Youth & Porn," https://enough.org, accessed May 10, 2019.

Fight the New Drug. "18 Mind-Blowing Stats About the Porn Industry and Its Underage Consumers" and "What's the Average Age of a Kid's First Porn Exposure?" Fightthenewdrug.com, accessed May 10, 2019.

Jones, Maggie. "What Teenagers Are Learning from Online Porn," *New York Times*, February 7, 2018.

Metz, Cade. "The Porn Business Isn't Anything Like You Think It Is," *Wired*, October 15, 2015.

Pornhub. "Year in Review," Pornhub.com/insights, accessed May 10, 2019.

CHAPTER EIGHT: BOYS AND BODY IMAGE

American Society of Plastic Surgeons. "Plastic Surgery Statistics," accessed May 10, 2019, www.plasticsurgery.org/news/plastic-surgery-statistics.

Centers for Disease Control and Prevention. "Overweight and Obesity," www.cdc.gov/obesity/data/adult.html. Accessed May 10, 2019.

Credos. "Picture of Health?" adassoc.org.uk, 2016, www.adassoc.org.uk/wp-content/uploads/2016/08/Picture-of-health_FINAL.pdf.

Drexler, Peggy. "The Impact of Negative Body Image on Boys," *Psychology Today*, January 17, 2013, www.psychologytoday.com/us/blog/our-gender-ourselves/201301/the-impact-negative-body-image-boys.

Field, Alison E., Kendrin R. Sonneville, Ross D. Crosby, et al. "Prospective Associations of Concerns About Physique and the Development of Obesity, Binge Drinking, and Drug Use Among Adolescent Boys and Young Adult Men," *JAMA Pediatrics*, vol. 168, no. 1 (2014): 34–39.

Hales, Craig M., Margaret D. Carroll, Cheryl D. Fryar, and Cynthia L. Ogden. "Prevalence of Obesity Among Adults and Youth: United States, 2015–2016," *NCHS Data Brief*, no. 288 (October 2017), www.cdc.gov/nchs/data/databriefs/db288.pdf.

Hudson, James I., Eva Hiripi, and Ronald C. Kessler. "The Prevalence and Correlates of Eating Disorders in the National Comorbidity Survey Replication," *Biological Psychiatry*, vol. 61, no. 3 (2007): 348–58.

National Eating Disorders Association (NEDA). "Statistics and Research on Eating Disorders," accessed May 10, 2019, www.nationaleatingdisorders.org/statistics-research-eating-disorders.

National Institutes of Mental Health. "Eating Disorders," accessed May 10, 2019, www.nimh.nih.gov/health/statistics/eating-disorders.shtml.

NCD Risk Factor Collaboration. "Trends in Adult Body Mass Index in 200 Countries from 1975 to 2014," *The Lancet*, vol. 387, no. 10026 (2016): 1377–96.

Santa Cruz, Jaime. "Body Image Pressure Increasingly Affects Boys," *Atlantic,* March 10, 2014, www.theatlantic.com/health/archive/2014/03/body-image-pressure-increasingly-affects-boys/283897/.

State of Obesity. "Underweight Children—Consequences and Rates," accessed May 10, 2019, https://stateofobesity.org/underweight-children/.

World Health Organization. "Obesity and Overweight," accessed May 10, 2019, www.who.int/news-room/fact-sheets/detail/obesity-and-overweight.

CHAPTER NINE: BOYS AND ADDICTION
American Society of Addiction Medicine. "Definition of addiction," accessed May 10, 2019, www.asam.org/resources/definition-of-addiction.

Becker, Jill B., and Ming Hu. "Sex Differences in Drug Abuse," *Frontiers in Neuroendocrinology,* vol. 29, no. 1 (2008): 36–47.

Hosseini-Kamkar, Niki, and J. Bruce Morton. "Sex Differences in Self-Regulation: An Evolutionary Perspective," *Frontiers in Neuroscience,* August 4, 2014. DOI: 10.3389/fnins.2014.00233.

KENHUB. "Neurotransmitters," accessed May 10, 2019, www.kenhub.com/en/library/anatomy/neurotransmitters.

Li, Ming D., and Margit Burmeister. "New Insights into the Genetics of Addiction," *Nature Reviews Genetics,* vol. 10, no. 4 (2009): 225–31.

Sherman, Carl. "Impacts of Drugs on Neurotransmission," *National Institutes on Drug Abuse,* March 9, 2017, www.drugabuse.gov/news-events/nida-notes/2017/03/impacts-drugs-neurotransmission.

Szalavitz, Maia. "The Addictive Personality Isn't What You Think It Is," *Scientific American,* April 5, 2016, www.scientificamerican.com/article/the-addictive-personality-isn-t-what-you-think-it-is/.

Tomkins, Denise M., and Edward M. Sellers. "Addiction and the Brain: The Role of Neurotransmitters in the Cause and Treatment of Drug Dependence," *Canadian Medical Association Journal,* vol. 164, no. 6 (2001): 817–21.

CHAPTER TEN: BOYS AND GUNS

Campion, Edward W. "The Problem for Children in America," *New England Journal of Medicine,* vol. 379 (2018): 2466–67.

Center for Homeland Defense and Security. "K–12 School Shooting Database," CHDS.us, accessed May 10, 2019, www.chds.us/ssdb/category/graphs/.

Chatterjee, Rhitu. "School Shooters: What's Their Path to Violence?" NPR: *All Things Considered,* February 10, 2019, www.npr.org/sections/health-shots/2019/02/10/690372199/school-shooters-whats-their-path-to-violence.

Council on Injury, Violence, and Poison Prevention Executive Committee. "Firearm-Related Injuries Affecting the Pediatric Population," *Pediatrics,* vol. 130, no. 5 (2012): e1416–23. DOI: 10.1542/peds.2012-2481.

Curtin, Sally C., Melonie Heron, Arialdi M. Minino, and Margaret Warner. "Recent Increases in Injury Mortality Among Children and Adolescents Aged 10–19 Years in the United States: 1999–2016," *National Vital Statistics Report,* vol. 67, no. 4 (2018).

Della Volpe, John. "Attitudes of Young Americans Related to School Shootings and Gun Violence," *Social Sphere,* December 2018, https://static1.squarespace.com/static/5b651ae5ee1759e688f559d2/t/5c365e19898583acb0dfc79e/1547066927115/190109_SocialSphere_Gun+Violence_Dec+4.pdf.

Eiser, Arnold R. "Neuroplasticity, Repetitive Digital Violence, Mass Shootings, and Suicide: Toxic Content in the Digital Age," *Health Affairs,* February 13, 2019. DOI: 10.1377/hblog20192012.316635.

FBI. "A Study of Active Shooter Incidents in the United States Between 2000–2013." FBI.gov, accessed May 10, 2019, www.fbi.gov/file-repository/active-shooter-study-2000-2013-1.pdf/view.

Fowler, Katherine A., Linda L. Dahlberg, Tadesse Haileyesus, Carmen Gutierrez, and Sarah Bacon. "Childhood Firearm Injuries in the United States," *Pediatrics,* June 19, 2017. DOI: 10.1542/peds.2016-3486.

Fox, Kara. "How US Gun Culture Compares with the World in Five Charts," CNN.com, March 9, 2018, www.cnn.com/2017/10/03/americas/us-gun -statistics/index.html.

Giffords Law Center. "Statistics on Guns in the Home and Safe Storage," Lawcenter.giffords.org, accessed May 10, 2019, https://lawcenter.giffords.org/ guns-in-the-homesafe-storage-statistics/.

Gladwell, Malcolm. "Thresholds of Violence: How School Shootings Catch On," *The New Yorker,* October 12, 2015.

Global Burden of Disease 2016. Injury Collaborators. "Global Mortality from Firearms, 1990–2016," *JAMA,* vol. 320, no. 8 (2018): 792–814.

Glynn, J. "Guns and Games: The Relationship Between Violent Video Games and Gun Crimes in America," *Arts and Sciences Journal,* vol. 207, no. 7 (2016). DOI: 10.4172/2151-6200.1000207.

Gun Violence Archive, www.gunviolencearchive.org/.

Holland, K. M., J. E. Hall, J. Wang, et al. "Characteristics of School-Associated Youth Homicides—United States, 1994–2018," CDC, *Morbidity and Mortality Weekly Report,* vol. 68, no. 3 (2019): 53–60. DOI: http://dx.doi .org/10.15585/mmwr.mm6803a1.

Jenco, Melissa. "Study: Teen Boys More Likely to Carry Gun if Parents Disengaged," *AAP News,* March 4, 2019, www.aappublications.org/ news/2019/03/04/guncarrying030419.

Jensen, K. Thor. "The Complete History of First-Person Shooters," Geek .com, October 11, 2017, www.geek.com/games/the-complete-history-of-first -person-shooters-1713135/.

Karp, Aaron. "Estimating Global Civilian-Held Firearms Numbers," Small-ArmsSurvey.org, accessed May 10, 2019, www.smallarmssurvey.org/weapons -and-markets/tools/global-firearms-holdings.html.

Metzl, Jonathan M., and Kenneth Talia MacLeish. "Mental Illness, Mass Shootings, and the Politics of American Firearms," *American Journal of Public Health,* vol. 105, no. 2 (2015): 240–49.

NDTV. "More US School Shootings in Two Decades Than in the Past Century: Study," April 20, 2018, www.ndtv.com/world-news/more-us-school-shootings-in-two-decades-than-in-the-last-century-study-1840102.

NORC at the University of Chicago. "General Social Survey Final Report: Trends in Gun Ownership in the United States: 1972–2014," March 2015, www.norc.org/PDFs/GSS%20Reports/GSS_Trends%20in%20Gun%20Ownership_US_1972-2014.pdf.

Pappas, Stephanie. "Female Mass Killers: Why They're So Rare," LiveScience.com, April 3, 2018, www.livescience.com/53047-why-female-mass-shooters-are-rare.html.

Rapaport, Lisa. "Gun Deaths Rising Among White Kids as More Families Own Handguns," *Reuters Health News,* January 28, 2019.

Silberner, Joanne. "Study: Kids More Likely to Die from Cars and Guns in US than Elsewhere," NPR, December 19, 2018, www.npr.org/sections/goatsandsoda/2018/12/19/678193620/study-kids-more-likely-to-die-from-cars-and-guns-in-u-s-than-elsewhere.

Statista. "Percentage of Households in the United States Owning One or More Firearms from 1972–2018," Statista.com, accessed May 10, 2019, www.statista.com/statistics/249740/percentage-of-households-in-the-united-states-owning-a-firearm/.

Walker, Molly. "Are More Kids Dying in Mass School Shootings?" *MedPage Today,* January 24, 2019, www.medpagetoday.com/pediatrics/generalpediatrics/77610?xid=nl_mpt_SRPediatrics_2019-01-29&eun=g1087941d0r&utm_source=Sailthru&utm_medium=email&utm_campaign=PedsUpdate_012919&utm_term=NL_Spec_Pediatric_Update_Active.

Index

About the Author

DR CARA NATTERSON is a pediatrician, speaker, consultant, and *New York Times* bestselling author of multiple parenting and health books, including *The Care and Keeping of You*, a series for girls with more than six million copies in print, and *Guy Stuff*, the corollary for boys. A graduate of Harvard College and Johns Hopkins Medical School, Natterson trained in pediatrics at the University of California, San Francisco, and then practiced at Tenth Street Pediatrics in Santa Monica, California. Natterson founded Worry Proof Consulting to give parents open-ended time to discuss what their own doctors can't squeeze into a visit. She lives in Los Angeles with her husband, son, and daughter.

worryproofmd.com
Facebook.com/CaraNattersonWorryProofMD
Twitter: @caranatterson

yellow
kite

books to help you live a good life

Join the conversation and tell
us how you live a #goodlife

🐦 @yellowkitebooks
f YellowKiteBooks
𝓟 Yellow Kite Books
📷 YellowKiteBooks